Introduction & How To Get The Most Out Of This Book

Are you eager to start a coaching business? What is holding you back? Are you overwhelmed by the unknowns or the risk? Would a step-by-step guide be useful to you?

This book will ease you into the topic of starting a coaching business, the coaching industry, the steps to register a business, the methods, and tools you need to operationalize and market your coaching business.

> A Goal Without A Deadline Is Just A Dream.

We looked at other books that were "hands off" and decided we wanted to provide both: education and application. So, you will find definitions, explanations, overviews, and even reviews of coaching tools. But you will also find practical application through prompts and our most popular worksheets, used by thousands of coaches.

To get the most out of this book, consider these questions first:

1. What SMART goal (**s**pecific, **m**easurable, **a**ttainable, **r**ealistic, and **t**ime-bound) do you want to achieve with this book?

2. What are the biggest questions you need answers for to make progress in building your business?

You can use the table of contents in this book in combination with a quick "flyover" through the entire book to map out a specific project plan to work through the segments of the book that you want to use.

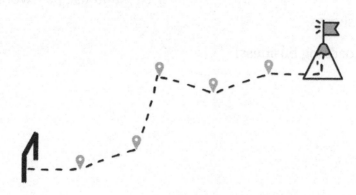

Then, select that topic from the table of contents and jump right to that segment. If you're a planner, you can take a piece of paper and draw a roadmap with the big milestones you're planning to achieve within a specific timeframe.

Think of this as a map that navigates you over time along the big mile markers to your launch. This will look slightly different for you than for other coaches and depends on your SMART goal.

The rest of this book will still be there to help you when you're ready to tackle the other areas. This way, you take one small step at a time.

If you want to get updates on the latest updates for online coaches, please join your peers and subscribe to Coachilly's community. You are on the right path to becoming the successful coach you're meant to be.

This guide covers five parts:

- **What is Professional Coaching?** Get a basic understanding of the coaching industry, what a professional coach does, the variety of coaching topics, and the audience seeking these services

- **Where and How Coaches Work.** Find out what path works best for you so you can make decisions on what to invest in and where to apply your energy and time.

- **Business Resources for Coaches**. Get an overview of industry associations, available education and certifications, templates, and software and technology to help you become operational quickly.

- **Establishing Your Coaching Brand.** Discover the basic principles necessary to start, grow, and maintain a successful coaching business and career.

- **Finding and Coaching Clients.** The last part includes a workbook segment and a checklist for you to implement the items covered in this book and start your business – step by step. For printable versions of the worksheets, go to Coachilly.com/coaching-startup-worksheets and use password "start" to access your worksheets.

Let's build your coaching business!

CONTENT OVERVIEW

WHAT IS PROFESSIONAL COACHING?

KEY DIFFERENCES BETWEEN COACHING, THERAPY, MENTORING AND CONSULTING

1. What is Professional Coaching?

Coaching comes in many varieties, particularly focused on life skills, business goals, career paths, educational paths, executive, management, health, wellness, relationships, and spiritual discovery. Relationship coaches focus on business relationships, friendships, parenting, marriage, and dating. The general description of a 'Life Coach' can include any or all the above areas.

The type of coaching you'll decide to provide is up to you, and depends largely on what your availability, preferences, skills, and knowledge can support. After many years of providing one type of service, you may want to expand your service portfolio.

Before you decide to branch out, let's dive into the state of the industry, and the requirements resting on you as a coach to serve your clients well.

The Coaching Industry in Numbers

In 2015 an estimated 53,000 coaches worked worldwide. This was reported by one of the certification organizations who only counted *certified* coaches.

According to IBIS World, there were over 33 thousand business coaching businesses in the United States of America at the start of 2020. In 2022, the number of registered coaching businesses reached 18,233. What's more, only 20-30% of coaches succeed. We'd argue that much of this is due to not planning well, lack of business acumen and not counting the cost and planning for few peaks and a lot of valleys to march through before reaching steady income.

The overall industry revenue in 2019 was reported at $15 billion worldwide, up from $2.4 billion in 2011. IBIS reported in early 2020 a continued 2.8% revenue growth in the industry each year since 2015. This rate had accelerated to 4.9% CAGR (compound annual growth rate) in 2022. By 2025, the U.S. self-improvement market is estimated to reach 14 billion dollars.

Some specific markets have seen more revenue growth than others. For example, in the United Kingdom, revenue grew by 5.8% in 2019, according to Entrepreneur.com's article, "How Entrepreneurs Can Join Europe's Booming Coaching Industry."

This continued growth has led to a boom in coaching-related research, professional coaching associations, coaching tools and software, and available training for aspiring or established coaches.

While the worldwide pandemic has slowed the economy, the coaching industry has quickly pivoted into the delivery of coaching services via online meeting and collaboration platforms. This includes popular providers such as Zoom, UberConference, or Microsoft Teams and through learning platforms like FreshLMS, Teachable, Thinkific, or Udemy that allow coaches to share their expertise with large audiences.

Coaches can be of any age; however, it can be more difficult for those under 25. As stated in the blog.marketresearch.com article, "U.S. Personal Coaching Industry Tops $1 Billion, and Growing," young coaches can find it "difficult to carve out a career in an industry dominated by professionals their parents' age: 37% of American coaches are 46 to 55 years old, according to the ICF." The ICF is the International Coach Federation, an organization aiming to set a high standard for professional coaches.

To overcome this potential obstacle, less experienced coaches seek education, training, certification(s), and integrate new technologies into their coaching techniques.

The Benefits of Professional Coaching

The easy way to define the value of professional coaching is to describe it as a coach assisting or guiding another person or group of people to reach their personal or professional goals. If you have ever gotten stuck or have fallen behind on your goals or your New Year's resolution for another year, you know how valuable it is to get help in breaking that barrier.

Many coaching clients have enjoyed additional benefits such as developing new habits, increased confidence, improved skills (communication skills, leadership, emotional coping, etc.), better decision-making, overcoming obstacles and limiting beliefs, and more.

The effectiveness of coaching is backed by research, including the 2015 HCI/ICF study Building a Coaching Culture for Increased Employee Engagement. The HCI is the Human Capital Institute, focused on human capital strategy. Results found that "60% of employees in organizations with strong coaching cultures were rated as highly engaged, compared with 48% of employees in all other organizations."

The Major Coaching Specialties

In the modern coaching world of the recent 40+ years, the "traditional coaching client" has been the executive. You may have also heard of a few celebrities working with coaches.

What used to be accessible and affordable only to an elite group has become mainstream as more coaches have entered the market for non-executive coaching in other niche markets. The push for quality through organizations like the International Coach Federation (ICF), which certifies coaches that follow their rigorous standards further drives the increased trust in the coaching process.

But what exactly *is coaching in the workplace*

Don't mistake coaching for consulting, mentoring, or career counseling. These disciplines are very different in focus and result.

What Is Coaching?

Let's begin this definition by contrasting coaching in the workplace with other disciplines often mistaken to be the same or similar.

Coaching is not counseling.

Counseling or therapy focuses on pathology. The underlying assumption is that there is a problem with the client that needs to be fixed and the counselor or therapist does the fixing. **Coaching, in contrast, considers the client healthy and capable and focuses on forward movement.** This shifts the focus from historic analysis and healing to awareness and growth. Counseling focuses predominantly on the past, coaching focuses on the future.

Coaching is not consulting.

Consulting puts the consultant front and center. The consultant is the expert who provides solutions or prescribes solutions. The underlying assumption here is that the consultant knows more than the client and thus is superior. The focus in consulting is on the object, not the person. **Coaching puts the client at the center.** A coach partners with the client to achieve the client's goals and assumes the client is smart and capable to derive actions her-/himself from the things discovered during a coaching session.

Coaching is not teaching.

Teaching puts the teacher at the top and creates unilateral communication. The teacher emits information and the student receives it. While there are "teachable moments" in coaching or adjacent services offered by a coach that include teaching, **coaching itself facilitates learning through coaching competencies** such as creating awareness, powerful questioning, and other tools.

Coaching is not mentoring.

Mentors meet with mentees on an informal basis and usually without a broad focus on personal development. **Coaching, in contrast, focuses on specific goals and follows a structured process with measurable results.** Mentoring is often indefinite while coaching is set for a limited time frame.

WHAT TYPES OF COACHING EXIST?

LIFE COACHING

All coaching is life coaching in its foundation. The competencies taught in professional coach training prepare coaches with fundamental coaching skills such as active listening, powerful questioning, and creating awareness, just to name a few.

Many life coaches break into niches to address the needs of their target groups. The most frequently named specializations are outlined below, but many more exist in an ever-growing profession.

Typically, those who explicitly state they are life coaches focus on areas outside of work in highly specialized areas.

Executive Coaching

Executives spend most of their workdays making decisions of significant impact, providing answers, and processing information from inside and outside the organization. Executives are expected to have answers and this expectation can limit exploration and growth.

Most often, the executive and the coach establish the connection. The request for executive coaching or leadership coaching is also frequently initiated by employers as the paying party, adding a level of complexity in serving two different stakeholders (contractor and service recipient). The overall goal is performance improvement and leadership development, with the client (the executive or emerging leader) defining more specific goals in the personal development plan with her or his coach.

The coach serves as a sounding board, helps with decision-making, uses the coaching process and various methodologies to bring awareness and clarity, and supports the client in creating action plans that achieve the executive's goals in her/his organization.

Emerging leaders often work on their communication skills, creating their leadership brand, developing their leadership style and executive presence, working toward their long-term career trajectory or upcoming promotion, and developing key leadership skills such as leadership communication and soft skills. To some extent, there is overlap with career coaching, however, executive or leadership coaching has a higher emphasis on talent development than career coaching (more below).

Business Coaching

Business coaching also focuses on helping business owners or business leaders reach their goals. It focuses more specifically on the leader's goals to grow a business. This is often more hands-on, with adjacent services focused on establishing or growing a business but can also include elements of the executive niche. Leadership development is often an integral part of the agreement.

Career Coaching

Career coaching focuses on employed professionals, job seekers, or those seeking a job transition in their careers. Adjacent services often include resume writing, interview training, and other job-search or hiring-related services.

This also includes mapping out a career path or creating a career development plan, working on personal growth, and job satisfaction, dealing with challenging situations at work, as well as long-term performance improvement topics.

As mentioned earlier, there is an overlap with executive coaching or leadership coaching when it comes to the talent development aspect. This includes topics of professional growth when a coachee (coaching client) requests coaching to develop important skills required for their continued professional growth.

Since the main emphasis of career coaching is on career advancement or transition to a different career, this professional development is often associated with immediate career opportunities or required skills to enable a career transformation.

WIDE RANGE OF OTHER NICHES

A growing list of other coaching specializations exists for other areas, including coaching in health and fitness, relationships, ministry, parenting, and in sub-categories within the above coaching areas.

For example, a Career Coach may specialize in a certain industry or focus on a specific career level, pairing their coaching with the teaching of practical skills for a specific profession or industry. An example could be teaching project management or sales skills as specialized career coaching niches.

ICF-aligned coaches follow a proven process, but they tailor each session to the individual needs of their clients and the flow of the conversation to maximize the impact of coaching.

A coach holds a client's agenda and makes sure that they stay on track during the call or meeting to achieve the objective they define for each call. A coach usually asks clients upfront which topic they would like to tackle or sends them a brief preparation form.

The Impact Of Coaching Backed By Data

The Benefits of Coaching

The benefits and tangible impact of coaching have been known by an elite group many for years. Now that coaching has become more widely known and accessible, people from nearly all walks of life have experienced the value of coaching.

In 2007, a survey from Clear Coaching Limited (PDF download) confirmed an extensive range of these benefits, including the impact of coaching on people through increased awareness, new or improved skills, better work relationships, ability to see others' perspectives, clarity in work life, increased motivation, improved atmosphere, increased sales/revenue, and more obtainable goals.

With so much added value and impact of coaching on people and organizations, the coaching market has been consistently expanding as individuals and organizations began to catch on.

The impact of coaching and the importance of staff development in businesses and at the executive level has led to most budgets including a line item specific to coaching for managers, leaders, or strategic planning.

Even Bill Gates and Eric Schmidt, leaders you'd think would already have it all under control, recommend coaching. Coaching in the workplace has found increased popularity as an article by Coachilly Magazine describes, because of the impact of coaching.

As stated by Tracy Sinclair in her June 2020 article, '*The Growth and Impact of the Coaching Industry*':

"Managers and leaders are using coaching as an integral part of their leadership style. According to the HCI/ICF study, 83% of organizations plan to expand the scope of managers and leaders using coaching techniques over the next five years.

Increasingly, organizations are including coaching training for managers and leaders in their annual budgets."

This demand for coaching is constantly increasing.

Of course, clients for your specific style and niche of coaching will vary, which is why you need to identify your buyer persona(s). These are the people that are part of your target market and interested in your services because they have the specific needs that you cover (see section 5 where you find a chapter and a worksheet helping you to create a buyer persona).

The better you know your target market, the better you can address them in a way that resonates. This will help you in your social media outreach and may also provide ideas about where your clients "hang out" so you can reach them there as a means of generating leads. Understanding the impact of coaching and articulating it well will help potential clients see the value you can bring, so let's take a look at the impact of coaching based on studies.

What Is The Measurable Impact Of Coaching?

Let's look at the impact of coaching based on research. The impact of coaching has often been hard to measure, for example, how do you measure the value of re-gained work-life balance? Luckily, many coaches, industry associations, and companies have realized this dilemma and the need to show the ROI of professional coaching.

As a result, we have a lot of ways to show the impact of coaching, specifically in the workplace (source: Zaradigm):

A Fortune 500 company did a study on the ROI of Executive Coaching and found:

- 77% of respondents stated coaching significantly impacted at least one business measures
- Overall productivity, employee satisfaction, engagement, and quality improved
- Overall, Executive Coaching produced a 788% ROI

The benefits of coaching for a team or entire organizations have also been measured:

The Harvard Business Review showed in an article that three stock portfolios comprised exclusively of companies that invest in employee development (such as coaching) had outperformed the S&P 500 by 17-35%.

The International Coach Federation (ICF) reports that "leaders who participated in coaching saw a 50% to 70% increase in work performance, time management, and team effectiveness."

Other studies support these metrics on the impact of coaching further:

- **6X** average ROI on the cost of executive and career coaching
- **72%** improved communication skills
- **67%** improved their work/life balance
- **53%** improved executive productivity
- **70%** enhanced direct report/supervisor relationships
- **67%** improved teamwork

THE TRANSFORMATIONAL IMPACT OF COACHING

As an article about the popularity of coaching in the workplace states, there is a reason individuals and organizations alike are hiring coaches. If training, workshops, seminars, podcasts, or books had the same transformational power, we would have little need for coaching. But as this Leadership Coach states:

Information isn't transformation.
I've spent decades in consulting, and in training.
The transformational impact of coaching is unmatched by other disciplines.
(Corinna Hagen, Leadership Coach)

Did you ever listen to a great speech or training or read a phenomenal book and thought it was life-changing just to find yourself unchanged at the end of the year? This is common and caused by a variety of factors, such as:

- Lack of creating a game plan to follow

- Lack of support to sort out hidden obstacles, or things you were unaware were hindering your progress

- Failure to dedicate time to your transformation

- Giving up early after not seeing enough change soon enough, or after a setback

- Receiving one-size-fits-all information, not a professional development plan tailored to your own challenges

- No help assessing and working through your existing approach, mindset, fears or hesitations, blind spots, relational dynamics, etc.

The International Coach Federation (ICF), the world's largest authority in this industry, conducted a global consumer study with clients. The chart shows the impact of coaching that clients reported.

For a general impact of coaching on clients, look at this chart showing the survey results from an ICF study. Things like increased productivity, confidence, or balance lead the chart in the impact of coaching and the associated benefits.

Figure 1: Impacts of Coaching; ICF Global Study

Not mentioned here is overall employee satisfaction. According to the International Journal of Evidence Based Coaching and Mentoring, executive coaching helps improve performance, satisfaction, and well-being. This is worth mentioning because many studies since the start of the COVID-19 pandemic have shown the correlation between employee satisfaction and other things impacting organizations, such as employee turnover and productivity.

The impact of coaching programs is often easier to assess and prove for a business coach, leadership coach or executive coach, career coach, or a health coach focused on easily measurable things like weight loss. But any life coach can also show the individual impact of coaching on the client by turning a coachee's current goals into S.M.A.R.T. goals by creating metrics. This will also allow you as a coach to collect proof over time to show the positive impact of coaching for your clients.

Why Famous People Recommend Coaching

From Bill Gates to Eric Schmidt, leaders you'd think would already have it all recommend coaching. A video summarizes their statements. Eric Schmidt dedicated an entire book to it. He also talks about a few benefits from his point of view it in his interview with Tim Ferris.

Great CEOs know they can get even better, as Eric Schmidt described. That's because they take on a role no one else has in your circles: they are unbiased, only interested in helping *clients* achieve *their* agenda, they have an outside perspective, and they have permission to ask tough questions that help clients to grow. Who else is contending for someone's agenda without having his or her own?

So, if these big shots have coaches, can everyone get a coach? Most likely. With the growing popularity of coaching and wider awareness of what coaching is and how it helps, anyone can find a coach on coaching marketplaces and other platforms for a rate that matches the level of coaching.

WHERE COACHES WORK

BUSINESS, CAREER, OR SIDE GIG?

2. Where and How Coaches Work

When choosing to be a coach, there are several avenues through which to enter the industry. This can include 'gigs' on the side, a career as a coach working for an organization, or your own coaching business. It is not uncommon to move between the three; however, it's most important to consider what will fit your lifestyle.

Let's look at some of the advantages and challenges of each model.

Coaching as a Profitable Side Gig

Well before 2020, gig culture in America was booming. Like having your own business, you locate clients through gig services or job postings. Many successful people start their business or pivot to new careers with a side hustle.

While it can take time to build your reputation and can be quite competitive, you'll benefit from being able to create your own schedule and crafting your own job profile. Once you have established yourself, you can determine your hours and income based on the number of "gigs" you can handle and how much you want to earn.

If you want to give this avenue a try, look for services on Fiverr, Thumbtack, LifeCoachHub, LinkedIn Services or Coaching.com. Fiverr and Thumbtack are one of the largest gig websites – or, in other words, platforms where freelancers find customers and business owners find affordable help for small and big jobs. For example, you could hire someone to write a blog post for you for a few dollars or hire someone for a bigger project like creating a website from scratch.

This can be beneficial for you where you need help in building your empire, but it also allows you to see what others offer and how they package their offerings. Let it inspire you and think about the services you could offer – perhaps in addition to coaching.

For example, if you offer lifestyle or health coaching, you may want to offer a meal plan that you'd only have to create once and can resell many times. Or, perhaps you want to offer a custom workout or meal plan for new clients who may consider coaching with you once they are hooked to your quality of service.

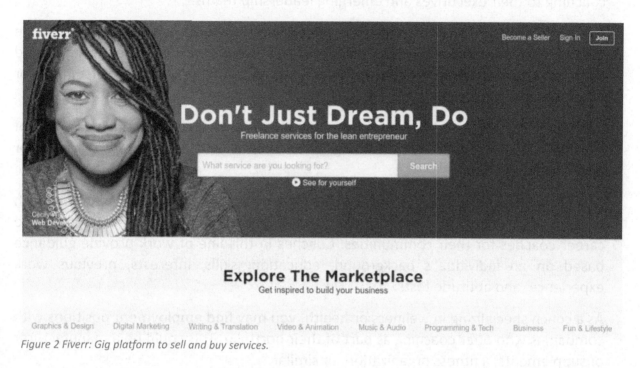

Figure 2 Fiverr: Gig platform to sell and buy services.

specifically focused on coaching services. Thumbtack is an exception, but it has a specific category for coaching, which allows you to narrow down results just to see coaching profiles.

Exploring these platforms can give you an idea of how other coaches position themselves, what they charge and how dense the competition is in your area of expertise or location.

COACHING AS A CAREER CHOICE

Some of the world's largest corporations have dedicated staff who provide ongoing coaching to their executives and emerging leadership teams.

These positions are highly satisfying and provide the benefits of employment: stable income, collaboration with other professionals, internal opportunities to grow and learn, and perks such as health insurance, paid time off, tuition reimbursement, or other perks.

In some cases, there can be a fair amount of travel involved, although the role of coaching is increasingly transforming into remote and web-based services for participants and coaches.

Nearly every school district, university, and higher education facility has a career coach or team of career coaches on staff. Many states and large city governments also have career coaches for their communities. Coaches in this line of work provide guidance based on an individual's background, education, skills, interests, previous work experience, and aptitude tests.

As a coach specializing in wellness or health, you may find employment positions with companies who offer coaching as part of their portfolio. This could be a manufacturer of supplements, a fitness organization, or similar.

The Entrepreneur Coach (Coaching as a Business)

As an entrepreneur, you have full responsibility for your coaching business. The success of your business depends on your decisions. You get to set your strategy, determine your messaging, and create your brand. You have creative freedom and to some extent can set your own hours. Only 'to some extent,' because you are not operating in a vacuum. For example, if you'd prefer working from 1pm-3pm every day and you find no customers to be available during that time, you will find yourself quickly adjusting your hours – unless your business is a hobby.

You have freedom to execute your own vision for your coaching practice. At the same time, you bear the full responsibility of running a business:

You pay for the software, hardware, products, or services you need to help you build and run your business.

You also wear many different hats to run your business:

- being the coach
- being the accountant
- being the assistant
- being the marketing manager
- being the "IT person"
- and all other roles.

As an entrepreneur, you must cover your own cost of health insurance and you are the sole contributor into your retirement savings. I cannot emphasize enough the importance of the financial decisions behind entrepreneurship. Starting a business without understanding the financial implications can lead to sudden and poor decisions.

One of the perks of being an entrepreneur is often seen as being able to set your own schedule. That is partially true, as already stated. You do not get paid time off like an employee. Your time off is your responsibility. It means if your business model is based on earning money in exchange for coaching (getting paid for time), then *not* working means *not* getting paid for that time.

Entrepreneurs are responsible for determining their own schedules. An entrepreneur coach has to set his/her own routine and have the discipline to stick to it. This is often very challenging for those who have depended on others to provide this structure. Since no one else tells you what to do and when (except the IRS), you must be able to operationalize your vision. This means that you must turn your vision into practical, day-to-day application.

Entrepreneurship is a discipline in its own category. Libraries are filled with books on this topic. To get you started, I highly recommend a bestseller by Michael E. Gerber, called The E-Myth Revisited. The book has been on the market for over fifteen years and has become a frequently recommended must-read.

The book talks about the three personalities inside every entrepreneur: (1) the visionary, (2) the manager, and (3) the technician. Entrepreneurs can lean too heavily on one of these three categories, causing them to neglect the other important areas of their business. I highly recommend this book if you decide to go down the path of becoming an entrepreneur with your own coaching practice.

Once you have made the decision to pursue this route, the following sections of this coaching guide will provide you with the information and worksheets you need to get started.

CRUCIAL SKILLS EVERY COACH MUST HAVE TO BE EFFECTIVE

You'll notice this section of the book is quite extensive. At Coachilly, these are the areas in which we assist aspiring coaches and skilled professional coaches from all walks of coaching life. All the training and certifications in the world mean nothing without acquiring the following critical coaching knowledge and practical skills:

Active Listening. Clients must feel heard and understood, which involves active listening on your part. Be mindful of what the client is saying, paraphrase it back to them, and ask clarifying questions. These build trust early on and won't result in assumptions, and everyone knows what happens when you act on (unverified) assumptions.

There are various ways of gaining active listening skills, but the easiest approach is to become genuinely interested in the other person and curious about what they can achieve.

Additional questions are necessary to fully paint the big picture, empathize, and consider the best option for the client. Coaches must be willing to put aside their own ideas about the 'best/right/obvious way' to do things and ask questions to elicit ideas about how to approach an issue.

Constructive Criticism. Direct, honest, yet kind feedback is essential and needs to be presented without blame or judgment. As you coach a person, it is also important to ensure a fair amount of positive feedback along the way. When feedback is necessary to provide alternative ways of being 'themselves,' they will be more open to it if a foundation of praise has been provided.

Professional Presence. Be mindful of your 'stage' presence and how others see you. Whether your style is jeans and a polo or a professional-looking dress, it doesn't matter as long as it appears put together, clean, and neat. But this doesn't stop with your clothes.

An excellent professional presence will include a blend of self-confidence, poise, and control. Altogether, this allows others to perceive you as competent and self-assured and sends an automatically positive first impression.

Understanding Human Motivation. Every person has different triggers for motivation. They could be related to love, money, fame, recognition, or giving back, to name a few. Fully understanding what motivates someone is key to knowing which tools and techniques will help your client.

There are five popular theories related to human motivation. These are critical to understanding why people do what they do. No particular approach is necessarily the single best solution but familiarity with these models can help reframe and understand the root of a person's decision, action, or inaction. This is an essential foundation to build on, so to review:

Maslow's Hierarchy of Needs. Abraham Maslow postulated that a person would be motivated when her/his needs are fulfilled. The need starts from the lowest level of basic needs and keeps moving up as lower-level needs are fulfilled. This hierarchy of needs is as follows:

1. **Physiological**. Physical survival necessities such as food, water, and shelter.

2. **Safety**. Protection from threats, deprivation, and other dangers.

3. **Social**. The need for association, affiliation, friendship, and so on.

4. **Self-esteem**. The need for respect and recognition.

5. **Self-actualization**. The opportunity for personal development, learning, and fun/creative/challenging work.

Hertzberg's Two-Factor Theory. Hertzberg classified the needs into two broad categories, namely hygiene factors and motivating factors. Both must be present to provide motivation.

Mcclelland's Theory of Needs. This theory focuses on the thought that we all have three motivating drivers, and they do not depend on our gender or age. One of these drivers will be dominant in our behaviors, stemming from life experiences. The three motivating drivers are achievement, affiliation, and power.

Vroom's Theory of Expectancy. Vroom believed that if 1) people believe it is likely that their efforts will lead to successful results and 2) those people also believe they will be rewarded for their success, that people will be highly productive and motivated.

Mcgregor's Theory X and Theory Y. This theory is based on the existence of X and Y people, which is based on their nature and requires certain kinds of management.

- **Theory X**: relates to people who are inherently lazy, self-centered, and lacking ambition, so they require a management style that is strong, top-down control.

- **Theory Y:** relates to people who are inherently motivated and eager to accept responsibility and need a management style focused on creating a productive work environment coupled with positive rewards and reinforcement.

Goal Setting. For clients to be successful, and hence, bring about your success, providing specific and attainable goals provides guidance and self-accountability for them.

The S.M.A.R.T. (specific, measurable, attainable, realistic, and time-bound) method of goal setting is widely used by professionals and is found to be effective.

Problems can also be turned into goals through reframing as described by Mark McGuinness in *Key Coaching Skills*, who stated, "...if a coachee talks about the problems he is having with a 'difficult' colleague, the coach might ask, "What needs to be happening for you to have a workable relationship with this person?"

Keep in mind that goal setting can be an informal process as well. It could simply mean defining one or two behaviors to incorporate into the life of a coachee as opposed to setting a big far-in-the-future goal.

In any case, goals mean little if they are not measurable and this part often presents the biggest struggle for both clients and new coaches. For example, your client may want to develop a new habit that is a contributor to a bigger goal. How do you track if the goal of "increasing my presence in the organization" is achieved?

You can look at this from different angles. One angle is to let others determine your client's progress by using a survey tool like the client's employer's 360 survey or their weekly or monthly reviews with their managers.

Another angle is to consider other "markers" that determine progress, for example building the habit of regularly speaking up in meetings or meeting twice a month with coworkers from different departments. Habits can be tracked by frequency (how often will the client do this, e.g., practicing a new habit), by outcome (results of an activity, e.g. positive feedback, agreement, etc.), or by the length of an activity (e.g., the amount of time set aside to practice a or learn a skill).

This last part can become a hurdle when clients – eager to create change in their lives – overcommit because they don't consider the effect such goals can have on their motivation to get started. If the time they plan to set aside is too overwhelming, they often throw in the towel when they miss their target once or twice. At that point, a coach may remind them to start small, with goals that are much more likely to be followed. A great example is the recommendation Wellness or Fitness Coaches often give their clients when starting a new workout regimen: Instead of committing to working out two hours every day, they ask their clients to commit to simply going to the gym (or leaving the house) in workout gear – no more. Just the act of leaving the house in workout gear has shown to be simple enough to make the habit sticky and powerful enough to follow through on some exercise.

Information Presentation. A critical skill for successful coaching is the ability to provide helpful, relevant, and useful information. Clients need context to help them accept, learn, and adjust their way of thinking, feeling, and reacting. The manner, tone, and materials you provide can allow growth and lead a client to expand their perspective or take the time to think through a situation.

At times, presenting a new idea may take a different and subtle approach. Though it may be obvious to you, you want to encourage the client to think outside of their own box as a coach. Simply asking the client how they could approach something differently can result in building their confidence and self-reliance.

Tread with caution here, because you will often feel tempted to simply share all the helpful things your client can do. Clients will also be tempted to ask you to give them "a list of things they can do" and while that's a tangible outcome you can help produce, don't forget that you are there to help them grow in a way that the client is self-sufficient and able to continue without you. We're not building crutches, we're enabling growth and transformation so our clients can confidently continue on a new journey.

What you can do to support is share frameworks, concepts, provide a mirror, share worksheets, books, courses, videos, or other helpful resources to aid the client in understanding new concepts, progressing further after your call and to manifest the learning further.

Protection of Confidentiality. Being a coach means you will know things about people that nobody else knows. It could be something as simple as their childhood nickname or complex relationships they've had throughout life. Unless you have explicit permission to share, keep their information and details to yourself. An exception would be the moment a client indicates they are planning to harm themselves or others. That is a legitimate reason to refer to professional help since this is beyond the coaches capacity. It is in all cases vitally important that you establish trust early on, and confidentiality is a significant part of that.

Personal Success. The success you have had with clients will help you to share success stories that will further drive your business impact. In the beginning, you may not have a lot of that, but you can draw from personal and relatable professional experiences that you can use in your storytelling about how you have helped in a similar fashion. As you gain new clients, be sure to document successes and failures, and what you learned from each experience. Also take every opportunity early on to ask your clients to share their testimony so you can communicate it to potential new clients.

Ethical Guidelines. A simple statement or full policy will depend on your personal style. Having set ethics in writing will allow you to keep professional boundaries with clients and be held accountable if you cross the line. At the same time, it provides you the ability to explain how coaching works and what it is not.

ICF has a 'gold-standard' in coaching with a complete Code of Ethics statement, which includes ICF Core Values, Ethical Principles, Ethical Standards, and a Pledge.

The Code itself covers sections for responsibility to clients, responsibility to practice and performance, responsibility to professionalism, and responsibility to society.

Empathy. This could be grouped with active listening skills; however, it is an important ability. Authentic empathy comes from a genuine interest in a person and cannot be imitated.

From listening and watching a person, it becomes easier over time to understand what a person feels even when they may not fully understand their own feelings.

Understanding Nonverbal Communication. Someone's body language tells you a considerable amount about that person's emotional state and level of commitment. Yet, it's easy to ignore, especially when we are too focused on our ideas about what needs to happen next. Keep the following factors in mind when communicating with and listening to your client:

Facial Expressions. The most common nonverbal means of communication is through facial expressions. Human faces can make more than 10,000 different expressions and usually occur spontaneously. Smiling, frowning, and eye-rolling are the strongest and most relatable expressions.

Body Movements. Hand gestures or nodding can easily convey enthusiasm or excitement. For instance, we all know someone who "talks with their hands." It also includes actions that we perceive as nervousness or anxiety, such as involuntary tremors, frequent clearing of the throat, or a shaking leg.

Posture. The way a person stands or sits is a crucial element in how others perceive them. Someone who stands with a straight back and head held high exudes confidence, assurance, and strength.

On the flipside, a person who is slouched or facing the floor demonstrates uncertainty, indifference, or weakness.

When a client suddenly has a closed posture with arms across the chest, it could be perceived as resistance, boredom, or hostility towards the current conversation (or they are cold).

Eye Contact. An effective way to build rapport is by maintaining eye contact. Eyes can indicate interest, attention, and involvement. A lack of eye contact may be interpreted as disinterest, inattentiveness, or rudeness.

Paralanguage. This includes tone, speed, volume, and pitch. All of these can have a vast inference in the words being communicated, such as something being told in a sarcastic tone.

Proxemics. No matter where we live, proxemics has become a number one topic in fighting COVID-19 (though most know it as social distancing). This is more difficult to interpret now since it is based on how closely people stand to interact with each other.

During business conversations, keeping at least 6 feet apart feels unnatural and uncomfortable because of proxemics. While we don't want to invade a person's actual personal space (up to 18 inches), a more common 'business' distance is no more than 3 feet.

Physiological Changes. These are generally associated with anxiety, nervousness, or discomfort and can include sweating, blushing (or flushing), and teary eyes. When you notice a client physiologically changing in some way, it's crucial that you make them feel comfortable.

You could do this by simply making an observation like, "This seems to upset you." You can also share that you are noticing a shift in the client's posture by stating, for example, "You suddenly lowered your shoulders." Then let the client expand on that.

Avoid Distractions. Human conversations can wander off into other topics or dissuade from the issue at hand. It's like a dog fetching a toy and seeing a squirrel. The toy becomes obsolete at that moment. You do not want to make your client feel obsolete because you get side-tracked by electronic devices, pets, or other people during your session. So, make sure your work environment is free of distractions so you can maintain focus when you are in session with your client.

INDUSTRY ASSOCIATIONS TO BUILD YOUR COACHING KNOWLEDGE AND NETWORK

Professional and informal associations that support coaches vary from informal knowledge bases to formal certification and testing associations. The one that is right for you will depend on the level of support you need or want. You have the choice between formal associations or more informal groups focused on sharing information among peers. A few options include:

International Coaching Federation (ICF)

With over 50,000 members, ICF is one of the best-known in the coaching industry. ICF was founded in 1995 by Thomas Leonard, the originator of the modern concept of life coaching. Leonard was also the first to develop a code of ethics and credentialing for coaches. Over the last decade or so, the ICF has become the de facto standard for coaching. As of 2021, the number of ICF current members with an ICF certification was over 41,000.

The International Authority for Professional Coaching and Mentoring (IAPC&M)

IAPC&M was founded by and is run by professional coaches. Their primary focus is building, maintaining, and raising awareness, as well as working to promote best practices for coaching internationally and to provide value-added benefits to members.

The European Mentoring and Coaching Council (EMCC)

The EMCC has been around since 1992 and like the name indicates, is focused on European coaches and mentors. The organization certifies its members and has roughly 5,000 members.

The Worldwide Association of Business Coaches (WABC)

Founded in 1997, WABC is focused on business coaching and differentiates itself from life coaching in general.

The Christian Coaching Network (CCN)

CCN aligns with industry-standard coaching organizations such as the ICF, IAC (International Association of Coaching), etc., but it is faith-based for coaches who include a Christian focus in their coaching.

The Association for Professional Executive Coaching and Supervision (APECS)

Specific to corporate coaches, APECS has the stated mission "to ensure that in a complex world, organizations are enabled to use coaching and supervision to deliver ethical and sustainable growth." Membership includes events and resources.

Association of Coaching Supervisors

Founded by Edna Murdoch, author of *Full Spectrum Supervision*, the mission of this association is to add value to the industry by exclusively focusing on coaching supervision.

Positive Psychology

A community of coaching practitioners that serves as a resource and knowledge base. Their purpose is to help like-minded cohorts to develop practices, grow in expertise, and save each other hours of prep time.

The List Keeps Growing

This list is not exhaustive. It is hard to keep up with the many new organizations in this field. It is recommended that you begin with the most widely known – and respected – organizations. One such organization is ICF, which has been among the first to attempt to establish a professional standard in a profession that does not have any regulation to this day. Their efforts have been welcomed and recognized by corporations and other organizations around the globe and their certifications are now more widely recognized than they were at first.

CHOOSING THE BEST COACHING CERTIFICATION PROGRAM

There are plenty of ways to become a professional coach and there is no shortage in the availability of coach training programs. But which are the best coaching certification programs that are recognized and provide you with a solid foundation that helps you to advance in your profession as a coach? We have found the 10 best coaching certification programs among a sea of providers. This article helps you understand what to look for and narrows down the best coaching certification options.

> *"The biggest challenge facing coaches today is that untrained and incompetent Coaches are damaging the reputation of the industry. The coaching field is unregulated. No license is required. Consequently, anyone can call themselves a Coach.*
>
> *The profession is painfully aware that inept coaching makes the field look bad. Currently, there are more than 500 training and "certification" programs worldwide, and many of them will certify you if you simply pay them a fee."*
>
> *– Umesh Venkatesh in his 2019 article on LinkedIn*

Unlike most professional industries, it is true that no certifications, courses, or training are required to practice coaching. Yet, career counselors and coaches employed as regular employees are typically required to have a master's degree. It's quite a disparity.

Most coaches either have an industry certification or a related degree in the niche of coaching they practice.

There are many courses and training sessions to help build your coaching skills and knowledge. While you may be thinking 'why bother,' having a certification will further legitimize the perceived quality of your services and more importantly, equip you to deliver expert coaching. It will help your professional development, improve the client's coaching journey, widen your toolbelt and help you to drive the transformation your clients are seeking in working with you.

But how do you find the best coaching certification for your field? It can feel like the proverbial search to find the needle in a haystack.

How to Choose the Best Coaching Certification Option

If you're determined to have the best coaching certification to back up your skills, there is an ever-growing list of colleges, academies, and courses available. But not all are the same. Coach training schools differ in their approach and in the prices and outcomes you can expect, namely the number of accredited education hours needed for coaching certification and included mentor coaching.

To compare them, we recommend you look at the best coaching certification providers listed here and some others you may find listed on the ICF list of accredited schools. Then, use the form below to take notes and compare side-by-side before making a decision.

Evaluation Card

School Name	Name and URL of school	
Training Format	Online, onsite, self-paced, live, etc.	
Start/End Dates	Program start and end dates, application deadlines, times of classes	
Total Edu. Hours	Number of accredited education hours	
Approach	E.g. online courses, workbooks, practice hours	
Mentor Coach	Are mentor coaching hours included?	
Program Cost	What are the total program cost to "graduation"?	
Payment Plans	Are installment plans available?	
Scholarship	Does the school offer scholarships?	

You will learn that schools differ in the type of certification you'll get, in the practical experience you'll gain, the field of study covered, the onsite or online curriculum, training format, class sizes, the cost for life coach training, training delivery methods (online, live, onsite, self-paced, etc.), and many other areas. Once you have read through this segment about the best coaching certification, make sure you ask important questions when you research and filter each school of interest to you.

The International Coach Federation's Role In Coaching Certification

The International Coach Federation (ICF) offers Associate, Professional, and Master Certified Coach credentials. To apply for the certification, applicants must have 60 or more training hours and 100 or more hours of coaching experience. At the professional level, applicants must obtain at least 125 hours of training and at least 500 hours of coaching experience. To apply to the master's level, applicants must have 200 hours or more of training and at least 2500 hours of coaching experience.

As you will learn, many coach training institutes also offer their own form of "certification." We put this in quotation marks because our experience and conversation with hundreds of coaches over the years have confirmed that the certifications of these schools are not known or respected by those outside of the coaching profession. Your clients will hardly know the difference, however, the ICF has been able to establish a strong reputation that has gained acceptance in wider and higher circles, especially for coaches who want to work with enterprise clients.

The ICF is setting the industry standard for quality in coaching, including the quality of training coaches receive. To ensure the standard is met, ICF has listed accredited schools or training organizations that have been vetted and approved. Coaches who pursue highly sought-after certification with the ICF can find coaching education that will count toward the credits needed to apply for their certification, so it's worth using ICF as the starting point.

Since the list of education programs is long, we felt the need to highlight a few for you here to make it easier to find a place to get started. Next are the top-rated coach certification programs. These are ICF-certified coaching programs and are typically providing a life coach certification. In some cases, the name of the certification is specialized, e.g., executive coaching certification, certified career coach, and so forth.

10 Best Coaching Certification Programs & Training Organizations

Before we start with the list of the 10 best coaching certification programs, it's worth mentioning that none of these organizations are affiliates and we do not receive any financial benefit from mentioning them here. This list is based on our online research and opinion and aims at helping you to have a starting point and to know what to look for. We recommend you compare several schools in the field you're interested in.

1 • Institute for Life Coach Training

The Institute for Life Coach Training is being one of the best intensive programs out there. This is because it covers everything you could possibly want to know about becoming a life coach. In addition to having over 200 hours of classroom training, it offers electives that are free of charge.

These include topics like how to make money as a life coach and market yourself effectively online, and they even teach coaches how to start their own coaching practice. These programs are approved by the International Coaching Federation and count towards ICF coaching certification.

2 • INTERNATIONAL ASSOCIATION OF PROFESSIONALS (IAP) CAREER COLLEGE

The International Association of Professionals (IAP) Career College course covers a wide variety of topics, including how to coach individuals and groups, learn from other coaches, and resources, gain clients, and start a business.

3 • INSTITUTE FOR PROFESSIONAL EXCELLENCE IN COACHES (IPEC)

Institute for Professional Excellence in Coaches (IPEC) offers an extensive curriculum designed to provide coaches with the knowledge and skills necessary to become effective leaders within the coaching profession. IPEC's comprehensive virtual training experience includes live webinars, self-paced courses, eBooks, podcasts, blogs, and much more. All content is provided free of charge, and students receive ongoing support and access to mentorship opportunities throughout the process.

The organization's three distinct credential programs are designed to help professionals develop and demonstrate competency in areas such as leadership, management, supervision, facilitation, team building, conflict resolution, and more. Each program is based on a unique set of standards developed over decades of research and practice. Students earn three certificates upon completion of the required coursework.

4 • PROFESSIONAL CHRISTIAN COACHING INSTITUTE (PCCI)

The Professional Christian Coaching Institute (PCCI) also covers a range of coaching classes from the very basics all the way to coaching niche specializations. The institute is accredited with the ICF and has partnered with best-selling authors like Dan Miller, or Michael E. Gerber, and provides high-quality online courses from experienced and ICF-certified coaches.

Their Essentials program is a comprehensive program that equips new coaches with deep coaching fundamentals and provides an intensive learning opportunity through a combination of education, demonstration, online classroom, and practical application through peer coaching. The modular approach and high quality of content makes it easily one of the best coaching certification options.

5 • INSTITUTE OF EXECUTIVE COACHING

The Institute of Executive Coaching also offers training for coaches that is accredited by the International Coach Federation (ICF). They offer fast-track programs and comprehensive programs in various formats, combining online and face-to-face instruction.

Their 2-year program consists of four core modules: Foundations of Coaching; Leading Teams; Managing People and Organizations; and Advanced Leadership Skills. The availability of choices, the depth of topics covered, their close adherence to ICF standards, and the opportunity to join a fast-track program surely validate the institute's addition to our list of best coaching certification programs.

6 • COACHU

CoachU's Core Essentials offers a complete virtual training program designed to help you develop essential coaching skills. Their Core Essentials program includes over 77 hours of video instruction and interactive activities. You'll work alongside a coach mentor throughout the program, and receive feedback and support from our team of coaches via live chat, email, and phone calls. This is a self-paced program that typically takes six months to complete. CoachU also offers shorter programs and in-person workshops.

7 • THE HEALTH COACH INSTITUTE

The Health Coach Institute has been offering dual life/health coaching certification as an online program since 2010. This allows students who want to be health professionals to earn the Certified Health Coach credential and become a certified health coach while simultaneously earning the Certified Professional Coach credential. They are now the only organization in the world to offer this type of dual certification. Coaches interested in pursuing either of these credentials must pass a written exam and complete a practicum.

8 • INTEGRATIVE WELLNESS ACADEMY

The Integrative Wellness Academy is offering a Master Integrative Life Coach Certification program designed specifically for Wellness Coaches already working in the field. Experienced coaches get a comprehensive overview of integrative coaching concepts and practices, including how to apply them to clients, families, groups, organizations, communities, and cultures.

Participants learn about the core competencies required for effective coaching work, as well as how to build resilience, develop empathy, enhance communication skills, and strengthen client commitment. Wellness coaches also receive training in the art and science of group facilitation, leading to increased confidence and effectiveness in facilitating group processes.

9 - Radiant Coaches Academy

Radiant Coaches Academy is an award-winning holistic coach certification program. The curriculum is anecdotally based on cutting-edge science and business education that incorporates neuroscience, business, marketing, and neuropsychology into the curriculum. It is accredited to provide 65 hours of approved coach-specific training hours through ICF.

10 - Certified Life Coach Institute

The Certified Life Coach Institute offers a fast way to become a certified life coach. Their certification program takes just 3 days to complete. There are no exams, no books, and no courses to take online or offline. All you need to do is watch our training videos and pass the final exam. We mention this as the last option simply because we believe it is great to get a high-level overview of coaching, but will not equip you in the same way the other coaching programs do.

The Certified Life Coach Institute is recognized by the ICF, however, the amount of education you will get here will not add the needed hours to qualify you for ICF's widely recognized and esteemed coach certifications.

Evaluating The Best Coaching Certification Options

It's worth looking into the best coaching certification options for your field of coaching. To do that, don't just take our word for it, but take a look at the ratings of different schools online and perhaps consider running an online search for other comparison articles. You may find more detailed coverage for your specific coaching field, for example, the best coaching certification programs for career coaches.

INCOME EXPECTATIONS FOR PROFESSIONAL LIFE COACHES

Salaries, hourly rates, and speaking engagement fees vary depending on coaching experience, notability, and additional factors, such as your coaching niche or specialty.

Generally speaking, life and executive coaches working on a full-time basis can make between $32,000 and $75,000 annually according to Glassdoor.com.

Glassdoor provides insights about pay ranges by geography, seniority and even within specific organizations and has become the go-to place for job seekers to read reviews by current and former company employees. The annual pay range is likely related to salaried full-time employees with the job title "Coach."

Pay ranges for independent coaches can differ vastly from salaried coaches. Coaches who enjoy participating in large group presentations, work with sizeable business accounts, or have high-demand specialties can make well over $100,000 annually.

According to an article on the "Salary Range for Professional Job Coaches," Richard Eisenberg, a senior editor from Next Avenue, states that coaches can charge between $50 to $500 per hour. Career consultant and author ("Modernize your Resume" and "The Best Keywords for Resumes, Letters, and Interviews") Wendy Enelow notes that hourly rates average $125.

As your experience grows, so can your hourly rate, to an extent. Additional income streams like public speaking or authoring further influence your income. For example, a keynote speaker can charge anywhere between $500 and $100,000 depending on the event and number of attendees.

Career coaches such as educational, guidance, school, and vocational counselors earned an average base wage of $37,750 annually, as of August 2020, according to Glassdoor.

Before judging this lower salary, remember this includes benefits such as paid time off, medical insurance, social security, and retirement. In the September 17, 2020 news release from the U.S. Bureau of Labor Statistics, benefits equal at least an additional 30% of your wages. When benefits are added to the previous base wages, it totals $49,075 annually.

You can also decide to use online platforms to get clients and can use them to gauge what your peers charge for coaching areas similar to yours. Think of these platforms like eBay for coaching services – they are marketplaces where you offer your service and will be matched with clients looking for someone like you. Read more about it in this article on 'How Coaches Get Clients.'

You can also claim yourself or your business name on Yelp or Facebook and start building your reputation through those avenues, although this takes longer to build a clientele when you join the market as a coach without a reputation and without reviews to prove your effectiveness with other clients.

THE BASICS OF A COACHING SESSION

If you wonder what a typical coaching session looks like, this primer about the basics of a coaching session will give you a rundown of what happens before, during, and after a coaching session. You'll get a coaching session example of the flow of a session as we explain how to run a coaching session. We'll round this off with some key coaching fundamentals to remember.

This is intended to provide you with an *overview* of coaching session basics and what typically happens during a session, and important points to consider. It will *not* replace proper coaching education.

WHAT HAPPENS BEFORE A COACHING SESSION

Before you coach the client, a few things are required to be prepared. First, you can help the client prepare by thinking through what they want to focus on in your time together. An hour can go by really fast and you won't solve the world's problems in 60 minutes (or however short or long your sessions are). You can help your client by sharing prompts that help them prepare. This can be an email with 2-3 questions, a prompt via the coaching platform you are using, or a (short) worksheet or an online form that helps you to speed up the establishment of the coaching agreement. More on that below.

Example Of A Typical Coaching Session Flow

KEY LEARNING & ACTIONS

AGENDA

OPPORTUNITIES FOR CHANGE

DISCOVERY

MID-POINT CHECK-IN

Time segments are rough orientations, not strict rules. The flow will depend on the dynamics in a session and the coach's approach.

Second, you should review your notes from previous sessions to briefly check in with your client on progress made since your last meeting. This will help you remember what to follow up on before you get into the call. Scrolling through notes to catch up on your last session while you're on the call with the client will be a distraction to the client.

Lastly, seasoned coaches have learned to self-monitor their physical, emotional, spiritual, and mental states. Doing so allows you to remove all distractions and center your attention fully on the client you serve. For example, if something unpleasant happened to you earlier in the day, you will have to find a way to free yourself from being mentally or emotionally occupied with that unpleasant event – or, if that is not possible, consider rescheduling your session in cases of emergencies that need your full and immediate attention.

The Typical Flow Of A Coaching Session

To understand coaching session basics, we need to talk about the flow of a coaching session. A typical coaching session is divided into key parts that follow coaching fundamentals and the science backing the impact the underlying approaches have in driving successful transformations. Think of a coaching session hour as a pie chart divided into chunks for key things that need to be covered.

To keep this simple, you'll have a short amount of time, in the beginning, to establish the agenda or focus for the session with the client so you both are aligned on what you will achieve together. This is followed by a larger chunk of time reserved for discovery, another large chunk for ensuring the discovery leads to learning, greater awareness, and clarity and allows you to identify gaps and in the latter part to identify how your client will use these insights to drive actions that move them forward toward their goals. You'll close the call off by recapping key takeaways and creating accountability and commitment.

Establish The Coaching Agreement First: What's On The Client's Agenda?

As you saw earlier, you can help the client prepare for the establishment of their agenda for the coaching session through pre-session prompts. This is not mandatory, but a great helper in getting the most out of the time you'll spend together as it promotes your client's thinking about their intention for the call, and the outcome they are expecting from the call.

This is an important core competency for professional coaches. The ICF describes this as the *"ability to understand what is required in the specific coaching interaction and to come to an agreement"* by *"Establishing the agreement for the current session. What is it the client wants to work on today? What will make the next 30 minutes most worthwhile? Establishing a focus."*

Begin The Discovery

Once you have clarity on the coaching topic your client wants to focus on, you will begin to explore with the client. This is the time to ask questions that help the client discover hidden obstacles, underlying beliefs, and perspectives, and to create awareness around "what's going on" so they can gain the clarity they are looking for.

Help To Harvest Insights, Clarity, And Learning And Identify Gaps

Awareness brings clarity and clarity allows your clients to plan the next steps. So, during your discovery, you will listen for insights, like those "aha moments" and help the client to harvest those insights. What do their discoveries mean for them? How does it inform their behavior, thinking, or decisions? What are they learning about themselves, their environment, or the subject they are exploring? What gaps need to be closed to move forward?

IDENTIFY ACTIONS FOR CHANGE

Toward the latter part of the call, coaches typically help their clients identify meaningful actions that will promote the change they are looking for. This could be the start of a new habit, a conversation they need to have, more reflection on their part, setting time aside to practice, and so many other options. It is important that the client determines what is meaningful to them as it greatly influences their commitment to follow through.

CREATE COMMITMENT AND ACCOUNTABILITY

At the end of a typical coaching session, coaches ensure there is a forward movement by checking on the client's commitment toward the actions you had previously identified. Among all the possibilities you have discussed, what will your client commit to doing between your sessions? How will they stay accountable? What will they do if something wants to get in the way of their commitment, meaning, how will they safeguard their progress?

WHAT HAPPENS AFTER A COACHING SESSION

What happens after a coaching session largely depends on a coach's approach. You could decide to follow up a the midway point between your sessions as a quick check-in by email, via chat, or phone. Some coaches use the opportunity to do a pulse check by sending a post-session survey that is very brief and will accomplish two things:

1. The coachee briefly repeats one key learning and action they commit to taking.

2. The coach receives feedback on how the coaching helped the client and/or what could be improved.

The first part further manifests the learning through repetition and written expression. The second part is important for your service quality and allows you to make adjustments to best serve your client's needs.

Depending on how you set up your coaching agreement, this may also be your opportunity to remind your client to schedule the next session if they haven't already done so.

COACHING SESSION BASICS TO REMEMBER

Here is a brief list of coaching session basics to cover in your coaching sessions:

Establish trust. No trust, no progress. If your client doesn't trust you, they will not engage in meaningful ways that allow for discovery, accountability, and being challenged to grow, and the dialogue will remain at a surface level. It is your job to create a safe, supportive environment that promotes trust and conveys a safe space to the client. This includes your demonstration of integrity, confidentiality, respect, and support to help your client achieve their goals (not yours).

Establish clarity. Make sure you understand what the client is saying, feeling, and trying to achieve in your session. This involves asking questions and summarizing the answers in the client's own words.

Leave no stone unturned. Focusing on one area can leave others overlooked. As a coach, you can help to widen the horizon through questions like, "Is there anything else to consider?" or "Do you know enough to move forward on this?"

Adjust to the learning styles and communication styles of your clients. Ask your clients in your discovery call or initial coaching session how they learn and what works best for them. For example, a client might tell you that they prefer examples. Others may share that they prefer candid feedback and being challenged. Take note of it and incorporate it into your coaching.

Listen more than you talk.You are coaching, not teaching. There may be teaching moments, but neuroscience has proven that telling or instructing alone isn't what moves the needle with humans – it's allowing the coachee to come to their "aha moment" themselves, with the help of a coach's leading questions.

The better we listen, the better the questions we ask, and the higher the chances that our coachees will gain insight. Insight is what motivates humans to action, not instruction.

Confirm commitment. A verbal agreement is good, but only useful if your client is committed to taking action toward achieving their goals. During the session, listen for verbal and nonverbal cues.

Ensure accountability. Goals without target dates and actions remain dreams. Make sure you establish an action plan in writing with SMART goals (specific, measurable, actionable, realistic, and time-bound). The client owns the action and the goals, while you as the coach help the client stay on track and make progress.

The linked neuroscience article above also explains how insight motivates us to action, but the motivation lasts only a short time. To change or extend that time, it is important to set actions during the coaching session, toward the end. Ensure that the client writes them down and encourages sharing plans with others (where the topic permits it).

Celebrate and double-check achievements. You may not think this is critical, but achiever-type clients can get so involved in working on the goals that they miss acknowledging their achievements. Other times, you may find that the client marks a tick in the box when in reality, there is still more work to do.

When there is still dissatisfaction, lack of clarity, or hesitation to move forward, you have good indicators that there is more ground to cover. Ask probing questions at the end of each session, to "check the temperature" and see if your client is content with the result of the session or if there is more to work out on the topic.

Upholding ethical standards. In all of your work, whether before, during, or after a coaching session, coaches are required to uphold the ethical standards that guide our industry. While we have no enforcement for many of the ethical standards, breaching them has consequences for your clients, your reputation, and your business. For example, crossing the boundary to therapy when the client needs help from a licensed counselor can have devastating consequences that you are responsible for if you fail to differentiate coaching from counseling so your client understands the difference and if you do not refer your client when it's clear that they need therapy.

HELPFUL RESOURCES FOR COACHES

TOOLS, SOFTWARE AND TEMPLATES

3. BUSINESS RESOURCES FOR COACHES

There are many resources available for coaches, including industry associations, technology, articles, and courses. Some are free or low-cost, while others can go as far as any budget will allow (and more).

Since we have previously covered industry associations and educational resources to become a professional coach, this part of the book will dive into the basics every coach needs when starting a coaching business.

Later in this segment, you will get deeper into the technology you will need to start and run a successful coaching practice, especially if you plan to deliver most of your coaching online. If you are not the most technical person, don't shy away from that segment. This book aims at making this as easy as possible for anyone to be able to get started.

At this point in the book, you have likely decided to pivot into creating your own coaching business. The following segments and chapters will give you both knowledge and pair it with action through some helpful worksheets, checklists, links to resources and recommendations.

Pause for a moment.

If you want to get the most out of this book, take a planner and place it next to this book.

Take notes and plan when you are going to do the things you need to do to implement what you learn. Set a goal for every week and work in so-called _sprints_. That's a term from the software industry and refers to getting large amounts of work broken down into smaller segments that are bound by S.M.A.R.T. goals (specific, measurable, attainable, realistic, time-bound).

You know how the saying goes: A goal without a plan is just a dream. To lift your dream of having a coaching business into reality, you need a plan with committed actions and timelines. You don't have to move mountains, just rocks. A few rocks at a time will move your mountain over time.

STARTING YOUR OWN BUSINESS AS A COACH

If you tend to be more independent, enjoy marketing and sales, and have an interest in owning a business, building your own coaching business is a perfect option.

Why is it important to realize this? Well, think about what you are getting yourself into. A friend of mine once said he didn't realize that being a talented writer wasn't enough in the business world – not if you have your own business. Because when you don't work *for* a business that has a sales department, you *are* the sales department!

Beyond your coaching skills, you'll need strong abilities and skills in general business activities, organization, and client management. More importantly, you'll need to ensure you obtain a business license and register your business name according to your local, state, and country's regulations and laws. You can use legal services like Northwest Registered Agent, Nolo or LegalZoom to do so.

Another important aspect to consider when venturing out on your own is that you call the shots, meaning, you are also the only one accountable for your own success. There is no one else to point to and you'll often wish there was someone to share the burden with. You could consider finding a business partner to start and build together. This has advantages and disadvantages. The advantage is that you are not completely on your own. You'll get the experience, ideas and knowledge of more than one brain. You can combine your financial resources and benefit from the connections the two of you (or more) can bring to the business.

The downside can be the potential for conflict, missed expectations, slower progress due to the added feedback and decision-making process, and so forth.

In addition, consider the typical time it takes small businesses to succeed and make sure you have enough financial runway to cover your needs when income isn't steady. This can take 2-5 years, sometimes longer, sometimes shorter. What matters is that you are prepared to endure to success and don't have to give up because you run out of money too early.

Lastly, consider that healthcare costs are now your responsibility and that there is no such thing as PTO for entrepreneurs in the beginning. Until you can scale and/or create passive income streams, you get paid when you show up. As we say, "if you don't hunt, you won't eat." If you have read through all this and are ready to start your own business, let's dive right in!

Best Business Tools for Online Coaches

There is plenty to do with your coaching business, and you can manage a lot by yourself these days with the right tools. Chances are you are running all your promotions, marketing, and coping with all your social media until you can afford to hire support.

There are other things you can do to make your business run smoother and free up more time to spend with your clients and running the business and staying organized.

Many of these business tools have won awards and some are available at no or very low cost. Some may even integrate with your preferred coaching software platform - either directly or via a Zapier integration.

Your Website or Landing Page

A website is the best place to let people know where you are and include all the information your clients and potential clients need to know. You can connect it to all your other social media and newsletters.

The landing page acts as a guide for people when they come to your website. It should be easy to read and everything should be easy to find. People won't hang around very long if it's too complicated.

A great place to start is Carrd. You can get whatever you need for a great price. Keep it informative and simple. Make sure people know how to contact you as soon as they get to your page and they can easily see where all the information will be.

Your Company Registration

Registering your company has many benefits. It makes you look more legit than just calling your business by your name. There are also issues around filing income taxes, as you will see much better outcomes as a business rather than filing it as a personal file.

In case you do want to incorporate your business and separate your personal assets from your business, you could try Northwest Registered Agent. They are a legal firm supporting small businesses. Small, affordable fees provide you with business registration services and you will get reminders come tax time to file accurate documents with one or two clicks. Your clients will also see you as more professional and trustworthy.

Your Logo

A logo is more than just a pretty design to put on your stationery. It helps you create your brand and your business. Looka is a great site that requires no design skills at all.

Looka combines your design preferences with AI to make beautiful logos you'll love. Once you have your logo, use the Brand Kit to access 300+ branded templates, create custom marketing assets, build a website, and launch your business.

You want your logo to become recognizable and you want people to think of you when they see it. Find something that will be clean, professional, and fit your style of coaching.

Your Newsletter

Sending a newsletter is a great way to keep your clients informed and relay any information you want them to know. Try using Sendfox. There is a one-time fee and you have access to all the tools you need.

This site has everything you need except the high price that many other similar sites charge. You have access to unlimited automation, scheduled emails, and plenty of smart features.

Your Banners and Social Media Posts

Setting up social media posts and banners for your Facebook and website background don't need to be complicated. You can use Canva to find all the tools you need.

It's either free or a low monthly fee at the price of a coffee. In turn, you get an ever-growing design tool to create websites, flyers, schedule social media posts (and design them all in one place), design logos, profile banners, and so much more. Unlimited designs, patterns, colors, and a large photo library are included – the selection differs for free versus paid accounts (worth the money in our view).

Your Professional Email Signature

If you aren't using a signature on all your email correspondence, why not? Even people without a business use them as they are very easy to do. You can make one using your own features on your email or use one that looks much more professional.

You can use Email Badge and get the polished professional look you want. Style your email without the help of a designer and follow simple steps to add the signature to your Gmail, Outlook, Apple Mail and other accounts.

Your Webinars

One thing everyone has embraced over the past few years is teleconferencing, online meetings, and video chats. Even grandma has learned how to use her video chat.

Hosting a one-on-one session or a group session is easy. However, not all conferencing sites are the same. If your client is in a different country, they may be charged or have difficulty connecting.

Sure, there are free sites, but some of them don't work as well as they could. Zoom just had a lot of bad press because of its encryption. They are surely working hard on fixing that.

In any case, Zoom charges a monthly fee and you'll pay extra for extra functionality. Active Webinar includes all that in your upfront price. Make sure you check with each provider if they integrate with your coaching software provider. Zoom integrates with a lot of cloud software vendors, so it's worth looking into it.

SCHEDULING MEETINGS AND BOOKING

Scheduling meetings or coaching sessions can be a hassle. If you have clients in different time zones or who work various shifts, it can be a lot of back and forth to try and book something.

You likely have heard of Calendly. Tools like that allow you to let clients book themselves on your calendar during times you have set aside as available for them. This is extremely convenient as it avoids the constant back-and-forth email exchange to find a suitable time on your calendars.

Calendly has been around for a while and integrates with a lot of other tools. But it also charges a monthly fee if you want to have a decent feature set, like connecting more than one calendar, which most coaches we know, do.

Alternative scheduling tools have set themselves apart as more fitting for coaches by offering landing page templates that save you time to set up separate websites for different services. Others integrate with your CRM (Customer Relationship Management system and also offer group scheduling tools (Hubspot) or work best for managing a team of coaches (Trafft). Additionally, if you are on a budget and need basic features and all future upgrades included for one lifetime price (pay once, use forever), TidyCal is your choice.

For most coaches, we have found Book Like a Boss (BLAB) to be the most versatile scheduling tool. New coaches love it because it spares them the design of a separate website since it comes with easy to customize landing pages, allows for paid and free meetings, and enables you to create booking pages for meetings and services. Seasoned coaches like it because it gives them a lot more control than most other calendar services, including custom URL, embedding, integrations, scaling with teams, etc.

Lastly, if you have already set up a coaching platform (see the chapter on coaching platforms), you may have a meeting scheduler included with your coaching software and have no need for alternatives.

Some platforms, however, offer limited features and customization, so make sure you create a list of business needs before you decide what you settle on. Most coaches we know use their coaching platform to schedule client meetings and other scheduling tools for meeting with partners, peers, and prospects.

Manage Sales Leads

Sales leads are what keep you and your business afloat. How do you manage an ever-growing list of potential clients? You had all these conversations and your post-it note collection will soon become unmanageable. What do you do once you have 500 people in your sticky note list to follow up with?

You do the same thing you are doing now: you keep them organized with a sales funnel and reminders to follow up. Start this practice early to let it become a good habit. To manage your leads, try Hubspot. It's a huge time saver, includes a ton of features with the free version that you don't want to miss. And Hubspot integrates with a lot of other tools.

Hubspot has a mobile app, too. Think of it as your coaching phone book for current and future customers. Hubspot also allows you to connect to your email (so you can track interactions you've had) and other services.

Check if Hubspot has an agreement with your preferred coaching software provider. If they don't you can use tools like Zapier to link your data from your coaching platform to Hubspot.

You can establish a link with Zapier where your Hubspot CRM customer database is updated as soon as you create a new customer contact, e.g. in CoachAccountable and vice versa. It saves a ton of time and works beautifully.

Accounting

Your coaching software platform may provide what you need for billing and invoicing, but you still need to track your expenses and do some accounting to be ready during tax season to file your income taxes. One of the most popular and easiest accounting sites is Quickbooks Online.

Chances are you have heard of Quickbooks, as it is one of the most popular accounting sites there is. It's ideal for small businesses and can help you save a lot of money throughout the year and help you with deductions.

It is a low-cost account for the self-employed. It even lets you add your accountant if you want one to look over your records in the future or need help with your tax return. QBO also has a mobile app to keep track of your bills on the go. The app can help you to track mileage driven to your clients and deduct it from your tax bill, which is extremely helpful.

Social Media Marketing

Not a coaching tool but still a very useful one. Planning to post all your social media content is a lot of work. Many of these platforms offer a lot but don't always deliver.

Missinglettr does make promises and keeps them. If you have your content ready you can pre-set them to be posted on most sites. Missinglettr allows you to pre-set content to be posted for up to a year ahead.

Assuming you have the content, of course. Many things will change throughout the year but there will be items you can plan to post and they will just be there for your clients.

You need to get the attention of your future clients and Missinglettr does an outstanding job helping you to do that. Missinglettr will save you a ton of time and money and improve your content engagement rate and lead more people to visit your website.

Most Used Business Software By Coaches

There's a lot of business software to assist your coaching and other business operations (e.g., finance, marketing, etc.) while saving you time and money. Have you wondered what business software other coaches might be using?

Running all aspects of a coaching business by yourself can be demanding, but this list of business software used by coaches can help you to reduce this burden. The business software mentioned below is cloud-based, which means you can access any of the links from almost any device with an internet connection.

This list is comprised of business software categories that are frequently used by coaches (and other solopreneurs and small businesses) and most of them easily integrate with most coaching platforms as well. This is important because coaches want any business software to easily "link" into other software they use the most, so they can save time handling things manually and focusing more of their valuable time on coaching clients.

Let's look at typical things coaches do as small business owners or as solopreneurs. Since you have to wear many hats, you get to be the accountant, run the legal department, are the head of marketing, and everything in between.

While the listed categories below won't cover every single aspect of work you will possibly take on as you build your business, but it covers the most common needs coaches have when running a coaching business. Of course, the software and services we list below are examples of well-established categories. There are some well-known providers and some new market entrants who challenge the existing players.

When you consider starting and running your business, you will undoubtedly think first about how to get your business set up in the first place, which is why we begin with business registration or incorporation. When you begin to build your business, you also consider other things, like:

- How will I invoice my clients or collect payment?

- How will I keep track of all the clients I interact with?

- How can I make scheduling time on my calendar easier?

- Should I start a newsletter to build trust in my expertise? How would I do it?

- How do I keep track of my spending and income for accurate tax filing?

- How do I set up and manage my online presence? Website? Social Media?

- What is the best way to conduct my coaching? Via phone? Video? What tools will I use?

- How can I offer additional services, such as online courses?

You probably will ask more questions as time goes on and you discover other business needs and begin to look for services and business software to help you save time – and perhaps also money for hiring a person to do some of the work these things can do for you.

Based on the list above, these are the most frequently observed categories coaches look for when considering business software to save time running their coaching practice:

II Types of Business Software Coaches Use To Save Time

1- Registering and Incorporating a Business

This first category is a bit of an exception because we're dealing with an online business service, rather than mere software. However, we found it important to mention it first, because it is the number one question we hear in conversations with coaches who have never owned a business and are curious about what to do.

The most reputable providers we can recommend in good faith allow you to register and incorporate your business (e.g. form an LLC, Inc., etc.) within just a few hours: Northwest Registered Agent and LegalZoom help you to complete the work for you through legal experts. They are surprisingly affordable, too.

2 - Payments, Billing, Invoicing

Square or Stripe are reliable and easy business software to set up for payment processing. There are constantly new platforms emerging, each at different price points. We recommend starting with a well-established payment provider to build trust with your audience.

Ensure that the payment platform integrates well with your other software and places your finances in the hands of a proven solution that will save time and reliably handle money transactions for you.

3 - Appointment Automation or Self-Scheduling

Trafft, HubSpot, Calendly, TidyCal, or Book Like A Boss are phenomenal tools to help you reduce the back-and-forth of finding a good time to meet with your leads and clients. Simply link up your calendar and send a link via email or embed a schedule link on your website to allow clients to self-schedule during times on your calendar. Coaches love this because they no longer have to coordinate this manually. All you have to do is link your calendars and tell the software which times are available for booking. The scheduling tool will do the rest.

4 - CRM (Customer Relationship Management)

Consider Hubspot for easy and powerful contact management that has a powerful free version. Salesforce and Zoho CRM are alternatives for standalone CRM software. Many coaches also skip the use of a CRM tool in the beginning and use a coaching platform to keep a customer database. While this may be the easiest thing to do in the beginning, it is having severe limitations as the coaching platforms we know find their strength in facilitating coaching (no surprise here), and not in other aspects such as creating email sequences, tracking email open rates and responses, and so much more.

5 - Newsletters

When is the right time to start building your email list? Right away! That's because you build a list over time and as your fanbase grows, so does your opportunity to make those who already know your abilities and trust your expertise buy other services from you when you launch them.

Try Sendfox for the easiest way to send awesome newsletters to your clients. Other popular tools with higher price points and more functionalities are Mailchimp, ConstantContact, and Sendinblue.

6 - Accounting

Quickbooks online is easy, and affordable and you can add your CPA online to your account come tax season. It's better than carrying a shoebox with receipts to your accountant and also allows you to always have your financial insights visible. Freshbooks is a great alternative.

7 - Social Media Marketing Planning

Missinglettr helps boost your social media marketing, content distribution, and re-purposing of content. It also allows you to fill your editorial calendar up for an entire year in a matter of minutes, not days.

An alternative to that is the most well-known social media management tool CoSchedule. It comes with a wide range of powerful tools widely used in the marketing industry.

8 – Creative/Design Work

Canva is a phenomenal tool for creating marketing materials, social images, business cards, brochures, and even videos and websites without hiring a designer or having to have design experience! Their library of templates has grown drastically over the last few years. There is almost nothing you cannot do with Canva: presentations, Instagram reels, quote images, small videos, company brochures, and so much more.

9 – Videoconferencing & Business Phone Lines

Zoom, RingCentral, and UberConference, and many other web conferencing solutions allow you to share your screen, use videoconferencing, run online events with features like polls, breakout rooms, and a growing list of other features.

Zoom has massively expanded its features and even offers you to combine your account with a business phone number so you can have a separate line from your personal one. Their app allows you to make calls from any device – phone, tablet, or desktop – and even send text messages conveniently from your computer.

10 – Online Courses

Many coaches try to expand their portfolio by offering additional services to generate revenue streams. The most frequent choice is online courses. Consider using course creation platforms that help you to both create and host the course, like FreshLMS or TalentLMS (used by well-known brands) and offer you a marketplace like Thinkific to showcase your courses beyond the reach of your website to their large audience.

11 – Task Automation

This last category may not be on your radar when you start your business. But over time, you will realize that there are some repetitive tasks. At that point, coaches ask themselves if it's worth hiring a VA (virtual assistant) to outsource some of the work, or if there is a way to automate some of these tasks with the help of business software.

We recommend Zapier for linking specific apps to one another to automate tasks and save time. For example, you can save time to match each receipt manually to your expenses in QuickBooks by automating several steps to do this accounting task for you.

How To Determine What Business Software You'll Need First

You may recognize right away that some of these categories will save you time right from the start. Other categories may intrigue you, but you're not at the stage where you need them. Coaches who think ahead keep track of the tasks they perform repeatedly. It helps them make better decisions about which business software to buy and which offers to forego (there will be plenty coming your way!).

Reviewing regularly what you spend most of your time on that is repetitive and could be offloaded to someone else or automated will also give you more accurate features to look for when you search for "the business software for accounting" or other solutions.

COACHING-SPECIFIC SOFTWARE

Since 2018, we have tested and compared over a dozen coaching tools every single year. Each year, we updated the comparison and added and removed coaching software vendors. Among the reviewed providers were many valuable options; however, keeping your budget and actual needs of your business in mind before purchasing anything is important.

You'll find an overview of the basics we are assessing at the beginning of this chapter where we explain each feature and what you should pay attention to when scouting for a provider. **Further down, you'll find a summary of highlights for each online coaching software platform.**

We have run these comparisons for four years in a row now. The most notable changes are:

- Changes to the criteria or features reviewed in our comparison table intend to match the most requested and offered features on the market.

- Prices changed, but not much. It was surprising to see how prices did not change much, in some cases not at all, despite the economic changes.

- We have noticed an increase in quality and competition, with new entrants crowding the market and existing providers aggressively improving their feature set.

THE BASICS YOU SHOULD KNOW ABOUT COACHING SOFTWARE PLATFORMS

Being a life coach requires you to have a lot of knowledge in many different areas. You will be asked to help your clients with their jobs and careers, their relationships, and major life decisions.

Your clients will be facing any number of obstacles that you will be required to help them identify and then move past. You also need to be able to identify their unique skills and abilities and get them to embrace them.

But, as life moves on, we are constantly facing new challenges. The pandemic has been a perfect example. People all over the world had to adjust their lives to cope with change.

Many people had to change their jobs and abandon their dreams. More people started turning to life coaches to discover new options for making it all work in an entirely new way. The coaching industry had already been growing steadily, but this change sparked growth to new levels as even enterprises caught on and purchased coaching for their employees. What was once an exclusive service afforded by a small group of people became mainstream.

To run efficient coaching operations, coaches need to be organized, with systems in place to handle demand without disproportionate administrative effort. You're in the business of coaching, after all, not in the business of indulging in administrative overload.

That's why a coaching software platform is the best way for you to keep track of it all. But not all coaching platforms are the same, so you may have to review a few. Most platforms offer a free trial so you can test it out and see if it will work with your style and methods of coaching.

Coaching platforms vary in price, features, and customer service levels, so examine closely what you are getting for the price. Before you sign up for any coaching platform, create a list of your must-haves and contrast it with the features you can live without. This will help you review and compare apples-to-apples and speed up your decision-making process.

A Word About Multi-Sided Coaching Platforms (A.K.A. Marketplaces)

Some of these platforms allow you to showcase your services to find clients or help clients to find you. There are multi-sided platforms ("multi" because they bring multiple parties together: coach and client) that do just that. They help two parties find each other. Those types of multi-sided platforms do not provide additional features to run your coaching operations, such as invoicing or hosting and sharing of courses or worksheets and session notes.

A select few multi-sided platforms provide both: a way to generate leads through their "directory" and a way to manage your clients. Examples are in this article on "**Where To Get Coaching Leads Without A Lot Of Marketing**" and if you check out our deals page, you may find a promotion code or special offer from one of these companies.

15 Things You Need to Know Before Buying Coaching Software

Many of the online coaching platforms offer the same basic features, and some provide a bit more or a bit less in their free or lower-priced subscription plans. You will find some of the features very helpful, some to make little difference.

Why that matters?

Well, we recommend that you create your own checklist of features you absolutely must have to run your coaching practice efficiently and rank it against the nice-to-have features. Features aside, you should also rank the importance of expectations you may have regarding server location (more under point 2 below), customer service levels, and user interface.

For example, a coaching software platform you like may have all you want but has unreliable service during your testing. Would you still sign up? Or, say, you find one that has the features you want but doesn't look as "polished" in its design but has reliable service and customer support. Would you sign up?

Let's look at some of the features you should consider.

1. Content Delivery Platform

If you have content to share with your clients, you want that to go as smoothly as possible. This may include worksheets, images, videos, templates, and so forth. Customers may want to share content with you or a group, as well.

It helps to have a coaching software platform that allows you to store such things in one place.

What to look for:

- Does the platform allow you to enable access levels of content for individual clients and/or groups?

- What types of content are you permitted to upload?

- Are you limited in the amount of content you can store in your account?

- Can you easily organize your content into folders?

- Bonus: Does the provider offer free content or templates (example: free starter packages for career coaches) to speed up the setup of your business launch?

2. Share and Store Legal Documents and Sensitive Content

When you are in communication with your clients, you often have to share contracts, worksheets, and any other content you have created for your clients.

Trying to communicate all of that via email and store the files manually, you are missing out on a tremendous opportunity to save time. It is very helpful to have everything concerning a client in one place.

What to look for:

- How does the coaching software platform secure your data? How often is your data undergoing backup?

- Does the provider offer online signature capturing in your coaching agreements? This would save you time and money you'd otherwise spend on integrating a service such as Docusign, HelloSign, etc.

- Where is your information stored? Does the coaching software platform provider's country honor data privacy laws?

- Where are the provider's server locations? As you are testing, do you experience a lot of delays or quick page load, for example?

4. Invoicing and Payment Processing

Payment processing allows you to collect payments, whereas invoicing solutions merely send out the invoice for your services or products. It makes your life much easier if you can do both at once.

Most of you have used a separate tool for invoicing in the past. Payment processors like Square have come a long way to help with invoicing and even scheduling appointments, but then all my client records still live in separate places.

A note on compliance:

PCI compliance is a mandatory standard required for the safety of credit card processing merchants (you). It protects your client's payment information and is standard with integrated providers such as Stripe, Square, or PayPal.

If you are using a coaching software platform provider that integrates with these payment processors, you're all set. If your coaching tool provider offers its payment processing solution, you want to look for PCI compliance as you must ensure it through your chosen partners.

What to look for:

- What payment provider options are offered? Is your favorite payment processor covered?

- Does the provider collect any additional fees on top of the fees you pay for the payment processor?

- Can you create subscriptions for your clients?

- Can you offer payment plans?

- Are you able to create a payment and invoicing automation as soon as a mentee or coachee decides to sign up for your coaching program?

S. IN-APP SESSION NOTES

You probably write some notes during a coaching session. It helps you to see patterns, keeps you focused and listening, and uses the same verbiage the client uses. You can use your notes to mark important comments or ideas and keep track of actions the customer took away from the call or resources you had agreed to share with the client.

Keeping all your notes in one place and connected to each specific client helps keep you better organized and speeds things up considerably because you don't need to dig around for the right folder on your computer. You want to be able to access past notes right away while you are in session without being distracted.

What to look for:

- Can you create session notes?

- Do you have a rich-text editor (allowing you to format text by adding bullet points, headlines, bold font, etc.)?

- Can you elect to share notes with clients?

- Can you add notes to a shared document or other content?

6. GOAL SETTING & PROGRESS TRACKING

How will you and your client track progress toward their goals? How do you measure from week to week or month to month that your coaching together has moved the needle in the right direction?

This is where goal setting and progress tracking features come in handy. They provide a checkpoint and accountability, but also a way to determine whether you need to dig deeper to remove obstacles standing in the way.

What to look for:

- Can both you and your client create, view, and edit goals?

- Can progress be measured? How are results or current status displayed?

7. Scheduling

This booking tool helps with eliminating the back-and-forth to coordinate a time to meet and always needing to recheck your schedules. This way, you connect your calendar(s) and can even create standard meeting types with templates and then share the link with others.

They click on it and see your availability (you can block time) and schedule themselves at their convenience. Calendly even allows for payment collection, if you want to charge per single event.

8. Customer Communication

Does the coaching platform give you the opportunity to communicate with clients directly on the platform? This can be a substantial time-saver and helps to keep information neatly collected in one place: the client record or account inside your platform.

Many online coaching software providers offer not only a discussion board or chat feature, but also allow commenting on specific documents to keep the communication tied to the context.

9. Courses & Programs

Many of the online coaching software platform vendors now include a course feature. Before you compare this feature offered by a coaching software platform with that of a full-fledged course platform, ask yourself: What do you want to achieve with courses? Where in your coaching process do courses come into play? What do you want to offer your clients through courses?

Many coaching platforms also offer the creation of "programs." This is sometimes done via the courses feature to help clients follow a specific journey in parallel to coaching to achieve their goal in a mix of education and coaching.

10. Mobile Accessibility

This is often overlooked. Most of our world is still applying a web-first or desktop-first mentality while the world IRL has begun to view the availability of websites on mobile devices as a new standard. Open your email on your phone and click on links that haven't been optimized for mobile and you quickly get the point.

Coaching software providers who understand the shift toward increasing mobile use are providing one of two options to coaches:

1. A coaching app you and your clients can download and install from an App store, or

2. A "web app", meaning a mobile-optimized version of their online portal that does not require an app download.

Both have their advantages and disadvantages. What matters is that the offer of either one of these designed-for-mobile-access solutions improves your customer's experience.

II. Brand Customization (White Labeling)

Most online coaching software has always allowed custom branding or white labeling which is why we did not feel compelled to call it out. However, this is a popular feature and many platform vendors in our review

12. Videoconferencing

In a world used to Zoom, we may not think about this right away, but with so many subscription-based services, you can become quite fatigued from it all. These bills all add up. What if you could simply use the native, built-in videoconferencing feature a coaching software platform provides instead of a separate subscription? Only a few providers offer this option.

If native videoconferencing is not included with your preferred provider, look out for one-click integrations with your favorite videoconferencing tool. Ideally, the coaching software platform allows you to change your settings so that upon client scheduling, the videoconferencing dial-in information is automatically added to your invitation.

13. Group Coaching

Do you plan to scale your coaching to serve a wider audience through group coaching? Where do you plan to host the content for this group? How do you plan to manage discussions? Of course, you could try to leverage a free platform like Facebook, but you may find that some clients categorically reject the social media giant for highly personal interactions.

Using the feature within a coaching software platform also has the advantage that your uploaded materials are already in place and only need to be made accessible to a specific group. This would also allow you to keep conversations in a single place.

14. Information Security

The coaching industry is not tied to standards at the level of, i.e., healthcare with its HIPAA regulations. However, you still need to be aware of the safety of your customer information and your customer database being hosted well.

You want to make sure the information is encrypted at least with standard SSL encryption. Also, consider where the tool is hosted. Different countries have different regulations for data privacy and security, and you need to be compliant.

15. ICF Reporting

Of course, you can track all your coaching hours required for ICF certification in a spreadsheet. But why not generate this automatically with the coaching hours from your clients and go hiking with your friends instead?

Depending on your situation, these tools will prove to be more or less useful, but just because you don't need them now doesn't mean you never will. If you are using a free trial, try out all the features so you are better informed moving forward.

But now to the apples-to-apples comparison and individual review of coaching software platforms.

A Side-by-Side Review of 13 Coaching Software Platforms

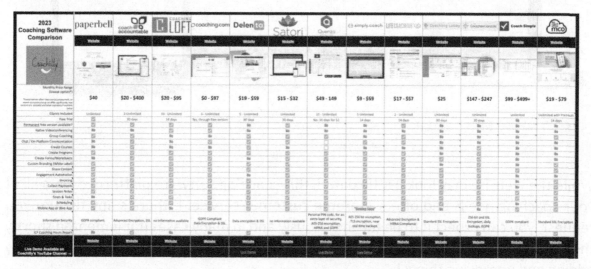

Figure 3: Coaching Software Platform Review - Link to Expand in the Appendix (Google Docs)

All coaching software platform providers listed here are randomly placed, **this is not a ranking**.

Make a list of items you value the most and use the review to help you down select a provider that suits your unique needs.

Some coaching software platform providers on this list are affiliates, however, none of the vendors listed anywhere in this article could influence their reviews. Opinions are my own and a contribution as a volunteer for Coachilly.com.

If you'd like to buy us a coffee for this effort, we'll get warm and fuzzy feelings of gratefulness and share a free assessment tool with you. If you'll leave a comment about how this helped you, that'll be rewarding, too.

COACHACCOUNTABLE

Figure 4: CoachAccountable

While the website may look a little dated, this coaching software platform covers all of your coaching needs and offers supreme customer service. If there's any feature you request, you can expect it to be taken seriously and in many cases implemented shortly thereafter, because CoachAccountable is quick to listen to customers and is constantly adding and improving things!

CoachAccountable has been around for many years and provides robust service and quality that makes organizations like Amazon, L'Oréal, Pepsi, Yale, and Standford University work with them (Enterprise account level). Looks like a safe bet to us!

Since we first began testing this coaching software platform in Q4/2018, it has added a ton of new features and made steady improvements. One remarkable example was our request for ICF report generation, a feature that John Larson, the founder, added within a matter of hours.

Highlights

- Starts at: $20/mo.

- Great features, intuitive interface

- Best client interaction and progress tracking

- Visually appealing user interface

- Customizable in very little time with white-labeling (make it look like your brand)

- Outstanding customer service

COACHING LOFT

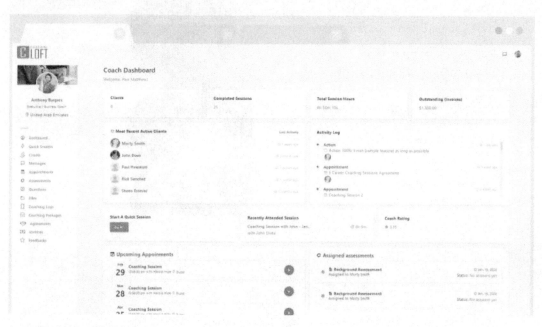

Figure 5: Coaching Loft

Coaching Loft has increased their features since our last review. This coaching software platform is highly rated on Capterra and has won awards. If I didn't already use a great platform, this would be my next pick. If you're looking for a great all-rounder that is decently priced, consider Coaching Loft.

Coaching Loft impresses as a great all-in-one coaching software platform. You can take session notes, send invoices, track client progress, schedule appointments, and more all from one single place. The interface is neatly organized and pleasant to the eye.

Highlights

- Starts at: Free, limited version

- Great user interface

- Reasonable pricing

- An impressive list of features that keeps growing

- A list of 500+ coaching questions

PAPERBELL

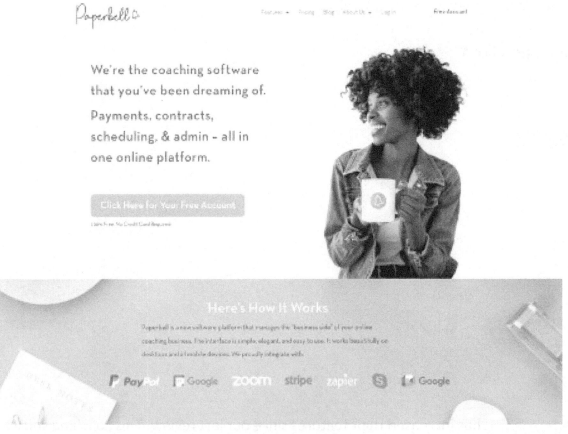

Figure 6: Paperbell

Paperbell strikes with a beautiful user interface, artfully designed. The coaching software platform offers an easy setup of packages for clients and fair pricing. They are designed solely for the unique work done by coaches and consultants. We've also noticed that Paperbell has partnered with ICF (the International Coach Federation). So, if you are an ICF member, look out for special benefits.

Highlights

- Starts at: $40/mo.

- Easy setup of landing pages, especially attractive to new coaches who may not need to set up a full website and can simply use Paperbell to create a web presence where clients can book their services

- Integrates well with other companies like Stripe, Paypal, Zoom, etc.

- Available in different currencies

- Secure via SSLDelenta

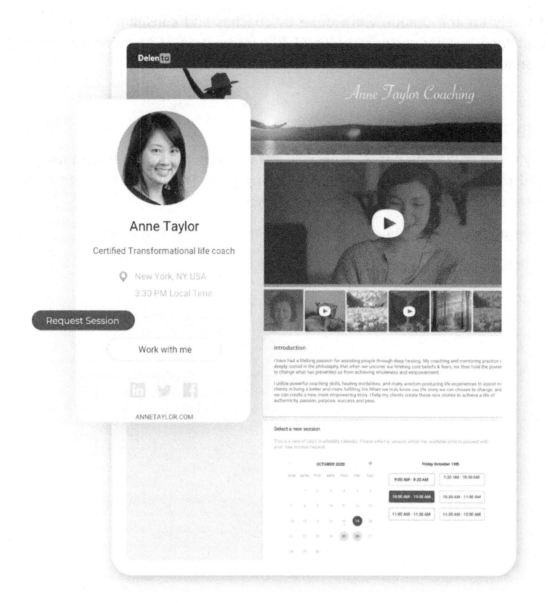

Figure 7: Delenta

Delenta impresses with its great user interface and the simplicity it provides. Since our last review, this coaching software platform has added a lot of new features like courses and a mobile app. Delenta wants to be your one-stop shop for coaching: you get to market yourself and run your coaching operations at the same time.

Delenta's software allows you to schedule appointments, invoice clients, exchange documents, and so forth. Also useful are the analytics Delenta provides to help you make decisions that help you grow your coaching practice.

Delenta became an official ICF partner – so if you are an ICF member, you get access to added benefits. Get more in-depth information and a replay of the Delenta live demo here.

Highlights

- Starts at: $29/mo.

- Attractive user interface

- An impressive set of features that leave no want

- Business analytics not seen anywhere else

- Courses

- Mobile App

COACHING.COM

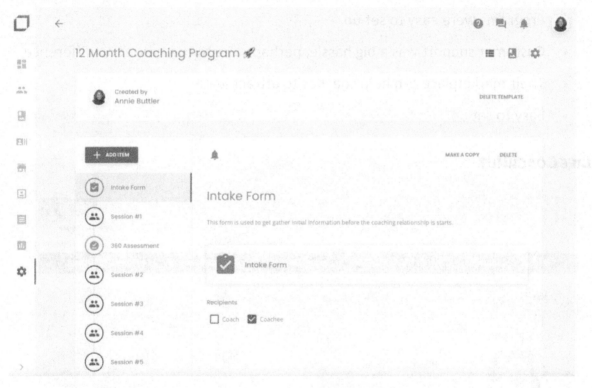

Figure 8: Coaching.com

Coaching.com (previously: CoachLogix) positions itself strongly in the coaching market by offering three attractive coaching solutions with its all-in-one platform:

1. A **coaching software platform** that allows coaches, enterprises, and coaching companies to cover all aspects of their coaching operations. This includes calendar management and allowing clients to self-schedule sessions, invoicing, sharing content, and billing.

2. A **coaching marketplace** that allows coaches to be found by clients and sell their offerings. Professional coaches can add their coach bios, offer their coaching engagements and give those looking for coaching an opportunity to easily schedule a first consultation with you.

3. **Continued education** via WBECS, a yearly coaching summit with high-profile speakers.

Like all of the providers we have researched since 2018, Coaching.com is a cloud-based platform. It does not require installation and is accessible from any device with access to a standard browser. You can view the honest, in-depth review of Coaching.com in this article.

Highlights

- Starts at: $0/mo.

- Impressive design

- Programs were easy to set up

- Customer support was a big hassle, perhaps due to the time zone difference

- Their marketplace can help coaches to attract leads

- Easy to set up

LifeCoachHub

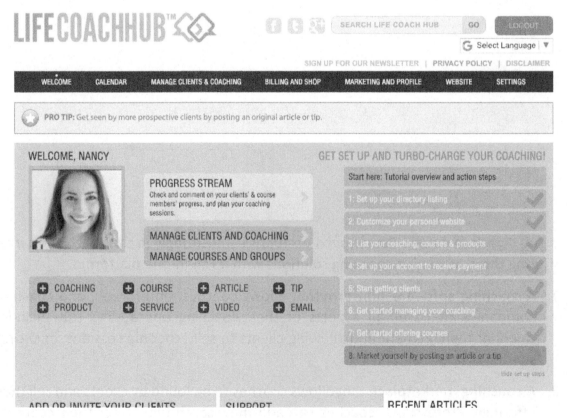

Figure 9: LifeCoachHub

Even before we reviewed this coaching software platform, we liked that it was more than a that. LifeCoachHub also works as a marketplace where coaches find clients and can market their expertise. LifeCoachHub has been around for a long time and was one of the first platforms to combine marketplace, web profile and coaching operations software in a single place.

For beginning coaches, this should be a great place to start as it allows you to work with clients, and promote your services in one place. If you don't have a website yet and need a simple solution to get you started, this place is for you.

Highlights

- Starts at: $17/mo.

- Integrated with a coach directory

- Easy website creation, a one-stop-shop solution

- Excellent online assessment forms in addition to the content library

- Progress tracking and client information is somewhat cluttered

SIMPLY.COACH

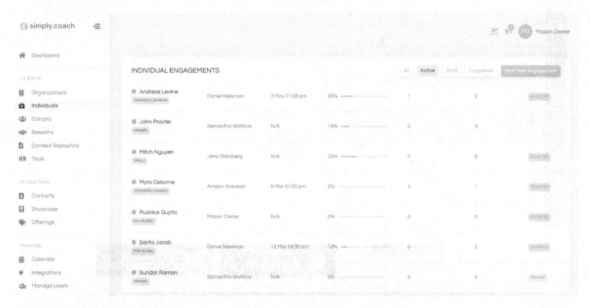

Figure 10: Simply.Coach

Simply.Coach is a coaching software platform based in India. It helps coaches to automate repeatable tasks so they can focus more on coaching and less on administration. A good example of this is their "nudge" feature, which stood out during a live demo we have recorded during our last review.

Nudges help coaches to predefine how often, and through which channel a coaching client should get reminded. In addition, they provide an attractive library of commonly used worksheets and journeys, called "pathways," which coaches can also create on their own.

Highlights

- Starts at: $9/mo. (individual coaches)

- Intuitive, simple user interface

- Attractive pricing model

- A unique approach to a coaching library (own + partner content to share with your clients)

QUENZA

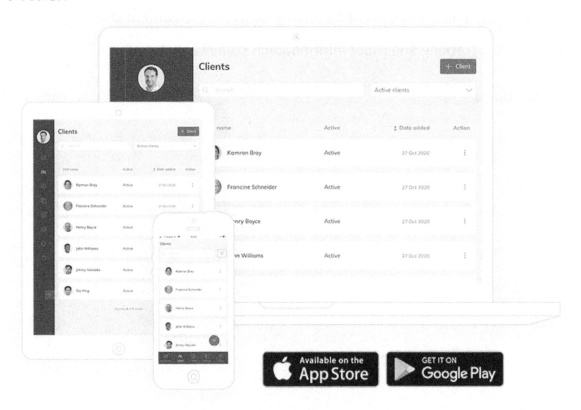

Figure 11: Quenza

Quenza made an impression with its interface and made-for-you approach: Quenza put a lot of effort into helping coaches to engage clients by helping to automate repetitive processes. In addition, this coaching software platform provides an attractive library of commonly used worksheets and journeys, called "pathways," which coaches can also create on their own.

Highlights

- Starts at: $49/mo.

- Attractive user interface

- An impressive set of features that leave no want

- Worksheets and pre-built customer journeys not seen anywhere else

- Higher starting price, but fair to say that it's also providing a ready-to-go coaching toolbox for newbies

COACHES CONSOLE

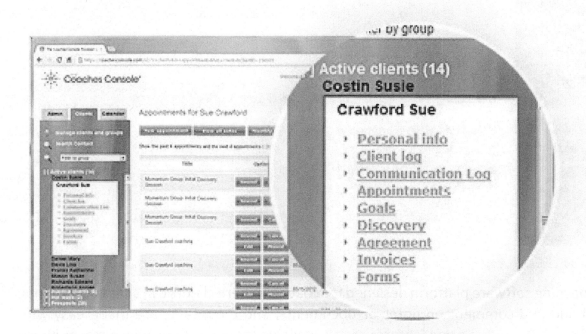

Figure 12: Coaches Console

Coaches Console's platform is one of the coaching software platforms that has been around for a long time and has a lot to offer. All of the criteria we've compared against are covered one way or another.

You can check it out for free to see what has improved or if you like the platform. Some people may like it more than other platforms. Use the free trial to see what you think.

Highlights

- Starts at: $147/mo.

- Comprehensive coaching software platform

- Great features

- Outdated design

- Highest price point

COACHING LOBBY

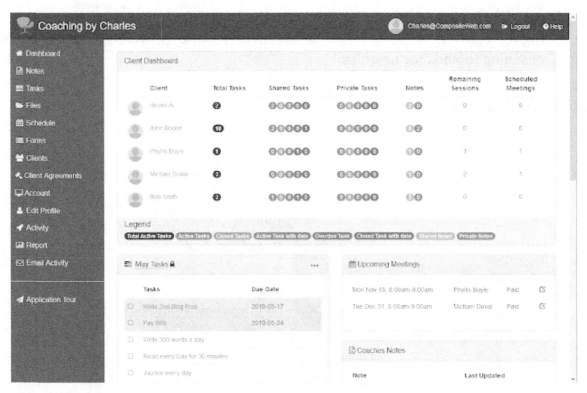

Figure 13: Coaching Lobby

A coaching software platform designed for coaches where clients can share documents, and add and comment on notes or documents, and most tasks are made easy with Coaching Lobby. The same features are all available for one set fee, which makes it nice as you are not pressured into buying a higher-priced subscription that you may not need.

The price is right, you have no limit on clients, and you can try it out for free for an entire month. If you are just starting out or trying to adhere to a tight budget, it might be the best choice for you.

Highlights

- Starts at: $25/mo.

- Easy brand customization (white labeling)

- A lot of features

- The provider's website did not include a video at the time of testing

- Not entirely intuitive coaching software platform

- One flat rate

My Coach Office (MCO)

Figure 14: My Coach Office

My Coach Office (MCO) helps you manage your coaching business from one coaching software platform. It is your all-in-one solution to enable you to deliver an amazing customer experience for every client without being a slave to administration.

You can use this coaching software platform on all your devices so you can run your business from anywhere. It offers one-on-one coaching or group coaching, so you can easily switch back and forth when needed.

Highlights

- Starts at: $24/mo.

- Sleek interface

- Highly visual progress-tracking

- Website updates are from 2016/2017 — which prompts the question of whether the software is actively maintained

- Only one-way document upload by the coach is mentioned in the feature description

- No information on information security is available

- Beyond Coaching Software

COACH SIMPLE

Figure 15: Coach Simple

Coach Simple's coaching modules are customizable to match your process and coaching style. They say they are enterprise-ready for scalability while simple to use for your team, clients, admins, and coaches. You can customize your programs with this coaching software platform.

Highlights

- Starts at: $99/mo.

- Sleek interface

- Highly visual progress-tracking

- Website updates are from 2016/2017 — which prompts the question of whether the software is actively maintained

- Only one-way document upload by the coach is mentioned in the feature description

- No information on information security is available

SATORI

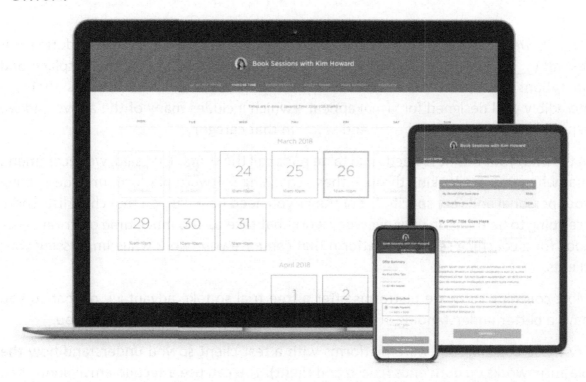

Figure 16: Satori

Satori has a lot of great features, including group coaching, personalized proposals, and signature coaching packages, where you can offer multi-session packages with agreements, intake forms, check-ins, and progress tracking.

Customize the theme of your booking pages and client login area to match your brand; and enjoy a beautiful, branded booking experience on any device.

One of the bonus features of this coaching software platform was the automatic follow-up. Satori follows up with your clients to remind them to schedule sessions, check in on progress, and provide reviews of their experience when closing out their program.

Highlights

- Starts at: $23/mo.
- One-touch client enrollment
- Clean and simple interface
- Custom branding made easy
- Optimized for use on any device
- Calendar integrations and timezone conversion
- Integrates with Apple Calendar

Selecting a Great Coaching Platform (+ Checklist)

Overall, we liked the platforms that provided the best customer sevice during our testing (CoachAccountable) and those that offer a combination of marketplace and operations tool (LifeCoachHub and Coaching.com). Next in line are tools that are incredibly well designed for visual appeal – which includes many of the above and we especially liked Delenta, Quenza and Satori in that category.

In the end, your business needs and taste buds call the shots. That said, we recommend that when you are looking through these coaching software platform providers, have your personal and very specific list of things you need help with on that checklist. There are going to be things in your everyday work that take up too much time or irritate you. Look for a coaching software platform that can ease your work while impressing your clients.

Most coaching software platforms offer a free trial so take advantage of that so you have a better understanding of how they work and how they will work for you.

Try these coaching software platforms with a test client so you understand how the platform works on both ends (coach and client). You can use a second email address to play the test client yourself. Some platforms give you a 30-day trial period. Make good use of it by planning your test cases. Simply put together a list of things you need to try, e.g., customers creating an appointment. A list like that will help you test in a matter of a few hours on most platforms.

This chapter hopefully gave you a good start to narrow down your choices. You likely won't need every feature we have examined in 2023 but that's quite common with any software. Ultimately, coaching software platforms are all about making your work easier. If they don't do that, then choose something else.

You can use the checklist to plan ahead and maximize your free trials with coaching platforms (or any software provider for that matter).

Software Checklist:
Try Before You Buy

- ☐ List the problem your software needs to solve

- ☐ Rank your list by importance

- ☐ List important features you need

- ☐ List integrations you need (e.g. calendar)

- ☐ Create a test case describing a typical scenario

- ☐ Find 3-5 vendors for testing

- ☐ Block time on your calendar for testing before signing up for a trial

- ☐ Sign up for trial

- ☐ Mark your calendar for end of trial to avoid automatic charges to your credit card

- ☐ Create a "test customer" using a spare email to test what your clients would see

- ☐ Test customer service, too!

- ☐ Check for promotions before signing up

- ☐ Decide for your favorite and leave a review for others

Coachilly

Templates and Tools to Start Coaching Today

You Need a Clear Coaching Agreement

A clear understanding of the services you provide and how much it will cost need to be in written form. While it's recommended you seek legal counsel for a contract template, there are various samples online.

Here's a checklist of what should be included in your coaching agreement:

O   Contact information for you and your client (address, phone, mail, etc.).

O   The purpose and goal of coaching.

O   How and when to expect payment, including any payment plans you may offer, flat fees or time-based charges (hourly, daily, monthly, etc.).

O   Rescheduling and cancellation policy with clear rules for cancellations and rescheduling of sessions.

O   Confidentiality and data protection.

O   The coaching process such as where and how the coaching takes place, expected time frame of the coaching, and how any support and interaction with your clients between sessions occurs.

O   What to expect and not to expect from the coach, including Information about methods and techniques that will be used.

O   A disclaimer that explains your client is responsible for the outcomes by implementing action steps taken from the coaching sessions and being collaborative.

O   Client responsibility statement to remind clients that they need to be accountable, act upon your coaching and do their part to make it a success and to accomplish their goals.

O   Disclaimer stating that coaching is <u>not</u> a substitute for therapy or medical treatment.

O   Cancellation policy with specific terms for both parties describing when and how the coaching relationship is terminated.

O Refund policy with explicit information terms regarding if and when you would offer a refund.

You Need A Session Prep Form

Before you start a coaching session, give your client an opportunity to reflect and gain clarity on what she or he wants to achieve during your call together. This will help you both prepare and makes the call much more efficient.

You can find a free downloadable template here.

A CoachAccountable account is needed to use these templates. You can register an account for free.

Use A Session Summary Form

While this is optional, it is highly recommended that you summarize the key statements and takeaways from your coaching sessions – at least for yourself. This is especially helpful once you have added dozens or hundreds of clients and thousands of coaching sessions behind you.

You can return to your notes in preparation for future calls or to refresh your memory (or your client's memory) on things you have discovered or worked on previously. People forget, but paper doesn't.

Some systems, like CoachAccountable allow you to store your session notes per client while also giving you the option to share your notes with your clients.

This can be useful if you covered a lot of ground and worked on an action plan. You would add great value to your client by sharing your notes while keeping your client free to focus on the call and on thinking, exploring, reflecting, dissecting, etc. as you coach and take notes.

Free Template Packages For Different Coaching Specializations

Once you have determined what coaching niche to specialize in, the following template packages are free and will give you a head start. These templates require the use of the CoachAccountable platform, which has a free trial version and a low starter price if you decide you like the platform enough to continue using it. Other platforms we have extensively tested have not been as flexible, reliable, and affordable.

You can read more about coaching platforms in the dedicated chapter in this book to help you evaluate which software will work best for you. But for now, here are free templates for popular coaching niches.

Free Templates for Career Coaching

This career coaching starter template pack includes:

- An automated onboarding sequence
- Predesigned courses for career coaching
- Worksheets
- Session templates
- Appointment types, e.g., full session vs quick check in

Free Templates for Wellness Coaching

This free wellness coaching template package includes:

- An automated onboarding sequence
- Predesigned courses for wellness coaching
- Worksheets
- Session templates
- Library resources to share with your client

Free Templates for Life Coaching

This free life coaching template package includes:

- An automated onboarding sequence
- Predesigned courses for life coaching

- Worksheets

- Session templates

- Library resources to share with your client, including assessments!

FREE TEMPLATES FOR FINANCE COACHING

This free finance coaching template package includes:

- An automated onboarding sequence

- Predesigned courses to promote coaching success

- Worksheets

- Session templates

FREE TEMPLATES FOR ADHD COACHING

This free ADHD coaching template package includes:

- An automated onboarding sequence

- Predesigned courses for ADHD coaching

- Worksheets

- Session templates

FREE TEMPLATES FOR RELATIONSHIP COACHING

This free relationship coaching template package includes:

- An automated onboarding sequence

- Predesigned courses for coaching success

- Worksheets

- Session templates

- Library resources to share with your client – including assessments!

FREE TEMPLATES FOR COACHING AGREEMENTS

This free template package includes five coaching agreement templates or coaching contracts you can modify to match your business needs and branding.

A Coaching Feedback Form

This is optional and doesn't have to become a complex chore. Keep it simple, but by all means, *ask for feedback every time*.

It will help your client reflect on the value of coaching with you. At the same time, you receive feedback on how you can improve or what you should keep doing to be a helpful coach.

☞ A free and simple 60-second mini survey template is available here.

Take the time to **create a list of what takes up most of your time** in day-to-day business. Then, rank the list by importance or time consumed and decide on a tool that fits your criteria.

Regardless of the popularity of a tool, don't compare yourself to your peers when selecting a tool for your business. The tool or options you choose must support the areas in which you need help.

As the coaching industry continues to grow, you can expect new and stronger tools to become available, including more customization so coaches can access 'modules' rather than all-or-nothing packages.

ESTABLISHING YOUR
COACHING BRAND

4. Establishing Your Coaching Brand

At this point, you may have completed coach training, or even become certified and are ready to begin coaching. Let's talk about what it takes to become operational as a coach.

Marketing your services is important to build your brand. **Customers won't find you if you haven't found yourself.** This means you need to have clarity on what you stand for, what you offer and don't offer, and your style of communication.

In the digital age, it doesn't require expensive marketing campaigns to find clients. You do need to learn a few things about communication, including storytelling, value-telling (also called value-selling in sales), and the use of keywords in anything you publish on the web. The last part falls under SEO, or, Search Engine Optimization, to be covered on a high level later in this book.

Creative Branding to Launch Your Coaching Business

Whether you use your personal name or have a clever business name, presenting a consistent message with your brand is important. This includes your logo and tagline. The tagline is a brief statement that states what your brand stands for. Look at examples of brands you know, and ask yourself, "what does this brand communicate? What emotions does it elicit in me? What draws me to them?"

Nike	Just Do It.
Intel	Intel Inside
L'Oréal	Because I'm Worth It.
Apple	Think Different
Allstate	You're in good hands.
De Beers	A Diamond Is Forever

In the same way, your brand will need to be able to draw your audience in and be memorable. Many coaches place a high emphasis on finding a clever name and forget the most important thing: the meaning of the brand, the actual brand association you are trying to build. That is more important than the name itself, because without absolute clarity on what you want the brand to stand for, all you have is a name. A business name without that is just a name, not a brand. To create a brand, you need your vision, your visuals, your services, your activities, your demeanor, your processes, the quality of your outputs and your communication consistently work together to portray exactly the brand you have envisioned. Your daily actions – whether in advertising, delivery of your coaching, social media posts, or other business activities – need to match that image. That's why it's called a brand image. It is the picture your external expression paints of your brand – visible to all.

Part 5 of this book includes a workbook segment to walk you through your business name creation. Once you have a name, you can use one of the many online design tools to create a logo. Looka has a simple, fun, and inspiring solution to create professional looking logos that look professional.

Make sure it's easy to read - both in color and when printed in greyscale. The lettering, colors, shapes, or images for your logo are part of your business brand. Anything posted, commented, or addressed with your name becomes part of your brand. Whenever you interact with leads, customers, business partners or just fans, your logo will be the visual representation of the experience you are working to create.

Once you have your logo design you are satisfied with, make sure you get it formatted for different purposes. Furthermore, you will need different sizes and resolutions of the image files. You will need your logo to be able to look consistent, no matter where it appears, whether in a circle (e.g., on many social media profiles) or as a square, whether you need it to be transparent or have a background, to have high resolution or lower resolution.

Most logo design tools already produce output in all formats and variations for you. A professional logo designer will do the same. Make sure you ask for the raw files (the original vector files) in case you need further editing later.

WHICH SOCIAL MEDIA PLATFORM IS BEST FOR COACHES?

The opportunities for engaging in social media are endless, but it's also overwhelming to consider being present on all of them. What social media platform is best for coaches? To answer that, we'll look at the differences between popular social media platforms and a few coaching niches and consider good matches between the two.

WHICH SOCIAL MEDIA PLATFORM SHOULD COACHES START WITH?

It is nearly impossible to manage more than a handful of social media platforms while building and running your business by yourself unless you can afford to hire dedicated staff.

The key to successful social media marketing in the early stages is this: whichever platform you choose, learn to manage it well and only add additional social media channels once you have mastered the first. Each social media channel portrays you and your brand.

The graphic below summarizes a handful of major platforms to consider for your social media presence, and why, including Facebook, LinkedIn, Instagram, TikTok, Twitter, and YouTube. For more details about the demographics who are using these platforms, take a look at the data in the Sproutsocial guide.

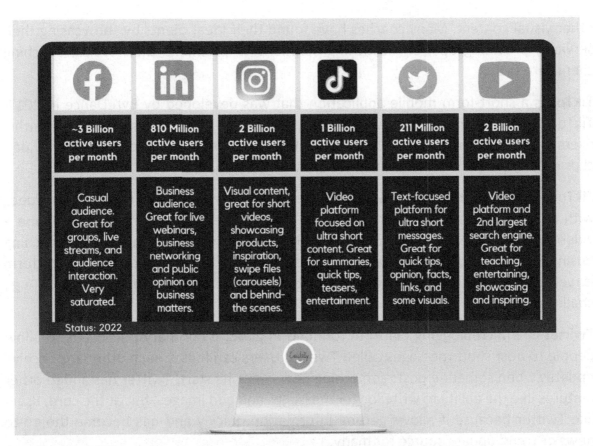

~3 Billion active users per month	810 Million active users per month	2 Billion active users per month	1 Billion active users per month	211 Million active users per month	2 Billion active users per month
Casual audience. Great for groups, live streams, and audience interaction. Very saturated.	Business audience. Great for live webinars, business networking and public opinion on business matters.	Visual content, great for short videos, showcasing products, inspiration, swipe files (carousels) and behind-the scenes.	Video platform focused on ultra short content. Great for summaries, quick tips, teasers, entertainment.	Text-focused platform for ultra short messages. Great for quick tips, opinion, facts, links, and some visuals.	Video platform and 2nd largest search engine. Great for teaching, entertaining, showcasing and inspiring.

Status: 2022

Figure 17: Social Media Platforms compared

DYNAMICS OF POPULAR SOCIAL MEDIA PLATFORMS

Facebook (Meta) is the most used social network with over 1.9 billion active users worldwide. It has been around since 2004 and was originally designed as a place where people could connect with their friends and family. Over time, Facebook began to grow into an online community where businesses could advertise and reach customers.

In 2016, Facebook introduced its own video streaming service called Facebook Live which allows businesses to stream live videos directly from their website. This feature has become very popular among brands because they can interact with their audience through live broadcasts.

LinkedIn is another social networking site that was created in 2003. It is primarily focused on professional networking and job searching. It is one of the largest networks in terms of members and companies. LinkedIn offers many different tools for marketers to use such as advertising campaigns, lead generation, content creation, etc. While not every business has a Facebook, Instagram, or other social media account, nearly all of them are presented on LinkedIn.

Instagram was launched in 2010 and is owned by Facebook. It is a highly visual app that allows users to share photos, videos, infographics, carousel cards or swipe files, and other visual content. Many coaches have found their ideal clients by showcasing their services, providing tips, or illustrating solutions to problems their typical coaching clients are facing.

TikTok is a short-form mobile application that was developed by ByteDance in 2017. TikTok's user base has been growing quickly. TikTok had around 2 billion active monthly users in 2022. TikTok is unique because it allows users to create their own short video clips called "Tik Toks" which can be shared with other people.

TikTok is different from other video apps because it allows users to create short videos with music and share them for free. Think of it as the Twitter version of YouTube – video, but bite-sized. Coaches have begun to catch on and promote their coaching business since the pandemic, but there is still plenty of room to grow as this platform is very receptive to experimentation with new content through prompts (e.g., challenges).

Twitter is a microblogging platform founded in 2006. Its primary purpose is to allow people to post short messages called Tweets. Users can follow each other and receive updates when someone posts something new. Since its start, Twitter has added other features like the ability to write longer messages and add images, but at the core, users like Twitter because it allows getting information quickly and has become the go-to news or trend update source for many.

YouTube is a video-sharing platform that was founded in 2005. It is owned by Google and is the second-largest search engine after Google. This is important: users no longer search for blog post results, but for explainers in form of videos as their second option to find answers.

YouTube hosts billions of hours of video content uploaded by individuals, businesses, educational institutions, and governments. This makes it the number one destination for watching videos. Many have used it effectively to promote their coaching business and establish their audience.

There are many more social media platforms, but we are sticking to the most popular ones as a starting point.

Which Is The Best Social Media Platform For My Coaching Niche?

The answer to this question depends on your coaching niche. If you're working with a seasoned demographic, then Facebook will work well for you since the audience has aged with the maturing of the platform. You'll have access to a large audience of potential clients, and you can easily target specific groups based on interests.

If you coach athletes, coaches, or parents, then Instagram might be better suited for you. The platform is specifically designed to help brands market products and services to consumers through pictures and videos.

For coaches who work with professionals, LinkedIn is probably the best choice. The platform is perfect for career coaches and business coaches to connect with other professionals. LinkedIn allows for various formats of content and provides those who don't have their own blog with the opportunity to reach a large audience via their newsletter hosted directly on the platform.

If you complement your coaching with teaching, YouTube is a fantastic way to teach clients with your expertise. The platform has become the second-largest search engine and a great way to showcase coaching services, increase your online presence, and build your brand.

How Many Social Media Platforms Should I Engage On?

When considering your first platform to create your business social media profile and showcase your brand, select the one that fits your demographic, matches the type of social media content you want to publish, and most interests you, because that's more likely to keep you actively engaged. Start with a single platform and master it before you add too many platforms at once. They all demand different content or formats and engagement styles.

Be selective about what you post but be consistent. If you start posting once a week, keep posting reliably. You will set an expectation with your audience, so don't disappoint them. Perhaps consider hiring a social media agency or a virtual assistant specializing in social media to get you started for success right from the beginning.

After all, the public will view your profile as an extension of your business. Regardless of the platform you choose, be sure to provide relevant, top-of-mind content, rather than copy/paste content that your audience will dismiss.

Unengaging posts will likely be ignored, so be sure to mix things up with emotionally engaging content, visually appealing content, small contests, free advice, and entertaining posts.

CREATE YOUR LEAD MAGNET

A lead magnet, you might have guessed it from the name, exists to attract leads. The better you address a pain point or a curiosity in your prospects, the higher the chances they will take interested in your lead magnet.

Typical lead magnets are free pieces of value for your client. This could be a free service (like a free first coaching session, a workshop, etc.), or content like a free checklist, a workbook, or an e-book. Anything you could give to you clients to showcase the value you can bring and to build trust in your abilities is a great fit for a lead magnet.

Especially for coaches with a well-defined niche, writing a specialized "ultimate guide" in the form of an e-book is a tangible way to solve a problem for your niche audience while growing your potential customer base. When an audience invests their time reading your work and learns something helpful, they are more likely to share it with others and come back to you for more.

If writing an entire book seems overwhelming or too time-consuming, reach out to a freelance writer to either assist in a draft or write it for you. If you decide to write your articles yourself, be sure to perform thorough research. Set your draft aside for a day or two, then read it as if you were a potential client.

Masterclasses or webinars are also great ways to showcase the value of your service to potential clients. This takes typically a bit more time to deliver than written content like an e-book, a checklist, or a whitepaper or case study. Those can be written once and passed along multiple times. The masterclass is typically an event you will have to repeat.

The opportunity for lead magnets is nearly endless, but their effectiveness will depend on (1) how well you address a particular need of your prospect, (2) the quality of your lead magnet, and (3) the placement or timing of your lead magnet. For example, asking right away for a free consultation before establishing some rapport may not yield good results. Consider at what stage of the decision process your prospect is at any given moment in your lead engagement stage.

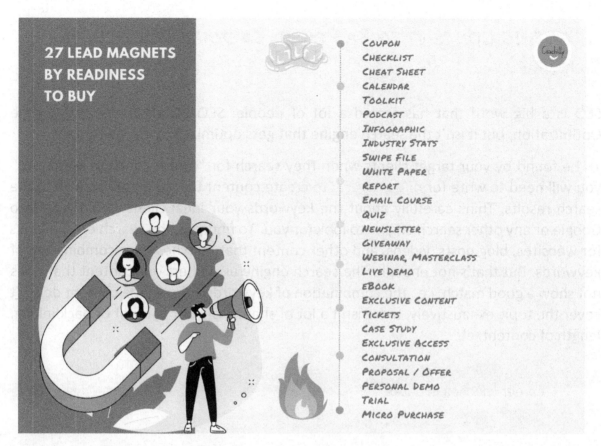

Figure 18: 27 lead magnets, ranked by readiness to buy

The following is a list of the lead magnets shown in the figure:

- Coupon
- Checklist
- Cheat Sheet
- Calendar
- Toolkit
- Podcast
- Infographic
- Industry Stats
- Swipe File
- White Paper
- Report
- Email Course
- Quiz
- Newsletter
- Giveaway
- Webinar, Masterclass
- Live Demo
- eBook
- Exclusive Content
- Tickets
- Case Study
- Exclusive Access
- Consultation
- Proposal / Offer
- Personal Demo
- Trial
- Micro Purchase

CREATING CONTENT TO BE FOUND BY YOUR TARGET CLIENTS

SEO is a big word that has scared a lot of people. SEO stands for Search Engine Optimization, but it isn't the search engine that gets optimized, it's your content.

To be found by your target clients when they search for "career coach in Memphis," you will need to write (or hire a writer) to create content that gets ranked high in the search results. Think carefully about the keywords your ideal client would type into Google or any other search engine to look for you. To find you, the search engine looks for websites, blog posts, videos, and other content that matches their combination of keywords. But that's not enough. The search engine also filters out content that does not show a good match, i.e., the combination of keywords indicate the content doesn't cover the topic exhaustively, there isn't a lot of sharing of your content or backlinking, length of content, etc.

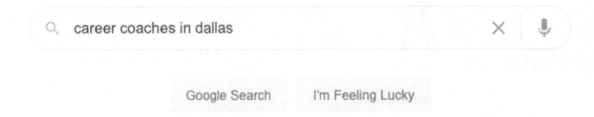

For example, the search above looks for coaches specializing in career coaching who are located in Dallas. If you were matching this category, you would only be found if your website matches those keywords. If you publish articles or blog posts on your website, include a brief author bio or byline at the end of your posts that states who you are, what you do, and how to reach you.

This will serve two purposes. First, it will establish your authority as a writer on the topic you just shared. Would you trust a lollipop manufacturer to give you a dental exam? Surely not. You may even suspect deceit. On the other hand, if a career coach is giving you advice on how to land an interview, you're more likely to listen to that advice.

Second, you will link back to you or your website. If you publish articles on other websites like magazines, or on LinkedIn, for example, the content is located outside of your own domain. This way, you reach a wider audience and get a chance to tell them where "home" is for you – your website.

To optimize your content for search engines (SEO), you can hire a writer to help you, or you can use tools that help you. Those are, in essence, text editors who give you advice on how to optimize your content as you write. If you were to write an article, you would upload it there or start writing it in that tool. You would then enter the keywords you are writing about.

To stick with the career coaching example above, let's say you want to write about landing an interview. "Landing Job Interviews" could be your three keywords for an article. An SEO tool will suggest better keywords if the market targeting those exact keywords is crowded. Throughout your article, the SEO tool will tell you if you use a good mix of headlines and keywords, as well as if you have good readability using paragraphs or lists, etc.

SEO isn't a topic to cover in a chapter or paragraph. A lot of work goes into SEO and results aren't instantaneous, but certainly important to pay attention to. If you don't want to hire an expert and prefer to dig in your heels, there are great free courses from well-established firms. This website provides a ranked list of 10 free SEO online courses.

To Convert Coaching Leads To Clients

How do you convert coaching leads to clients during your free consultation? You've done all the correct work of creating valuable content, and reaching out to generate leads, and now they are interested. But, for some reason, you only hear crickets after your free consultation with them.

For successful business development, your sales conversation needs to hit the mark. But how do you master your first conversation with a potential client (a.k.a. lead) so you leave a lasting impression that turns lurkers into fans and converts coaching leads to committed clients?

Attract Leads To a Free Consultation Before Converting Coaching Leads To Clients

Before you can have the opportunity for a conversation with a coaching lead, you need to make sure they can find you. There are several ways of doing this. A great way to do that is by sharing your expertise. You have several options here:

A landing page draws a person to your coaching service. This can be on a third-party platform like Noomii or Thumbtack or via your website. We have created an in-depth article covering everything you need to create a great website, including a website design checklist.

Your landing page should include information about who you serve, what your typical client looks like, and the challenges they are facing. An excellent landing page will resonate with prospects in your target group if it "hits a nerve" by addressing these challenges. You can use a worksheet to identify your coaching niche in six steps for better clarity on *who* you serve and *how* you need to articulate your offers to the right buyer personas.

Show how your coaching addresses these points. Include a professional photograph of yourself, testimonials from those who you have successfully coached, and a call-to-action (CTA). CTAs tell your visitors what the next steps are, for example, prompts like "book now" or "schedule a free call."

You can also embed CTAs like "book a free consultation" on your blog. This way, an article from you that resonates well with clients will provide a direct opportunity to get in touch with you.

How to Connect With Leads On A Free Consultation Call

Prepare Your Free Consultation

In a nutshell, free consultation in coaching is a call –ranging between 15 minutes and 60 minutes. Your client provides an introduction of what leads them to look for a coach at this time. You introduce yourself and answer questions your potential client may have.

Some free consultations include a brief sample of coaching to showcase what coaching would look like with you. Whether you include this or not, you need to clarify what you offer and listen well to your prospects to understand what they are looking for.

Before the call, take the time to prepare:

- What do you need to know from the potential client?

- What information do you need to provide?

- What should happen when the call ends?

- Will you share pricing before, during, or after the call?

There should be a natural flow to the call, and you'll want to ensure a focused conversation to understand your client's needs. At the end of the call, be sure that you have met their expectations for the call, which requires that you listen well – more on that next.

Listen First

Keep the free consultation specific to the needs of the interested person. Ask first about their needs *before* going into a presentation or pitch of what you offer. This consultation is about them, first.

Ask clarifying questions if needed. Make sure you understand your coaching lead's challenges before sharing how you can help. Repeat what they have said to you about their needs to ensure you have correctly understood them and to build trust. This will allow you to explain your services contextually. The better you can connect your coaching services to your prospective client's needs, the more likely you will have a great free consultation that will convert coaching leads to clients.

The more you listen and ask discovery questions to learn about the client's needs, the higher your likelihood to be *relevant* to the client as you articulate how your coaching helps the client.

Listen more than you explain. This conversation is first about the client, and second about you. Put the client at the center and hold your tongue until you understand the concerns and needs of your client well enough to create a relatable response that shows the client that you understand them and can signal them that you can help. The best prompt is one created by the coaching lead when they ask you directly to explain if and how you could help them.

CONSIDER OFFERING A GIFT

By offering something of value to your prospect, you can show what you bring to the table. It is also an effective and widely used sales tool because *we are wired to return favors* – not any favor, but meaningful favors. So, think of the value you can offer to your potential client here. You don't have to give away everything you've worked so hard to create. Think about something most of your clients need and create a lead magnet. Many businesses provide lead magnets as free downloads in exchange for an email address or a phone consultation.

To come up with ideas for the needs of your clients and what they are looking for, consider using audience research tools like Answer The Public. Type in a keyword you want to represent, a topic you specialize in, and explore what options come up. It will tell you what your ideal client is looking for and what they are typing into the search engine to find you.

Alternatively, you can compile a list of helpful information you can send as a follow-up after the free consultation. As a Health Coach, this may be a recipe or food list. As a Career Coach, this may be a template, a checklist, or a list of resources. In some cases, your lead magnet could even serve as a worksheet for events or to be used during your free consultation to map out a rough plan that your leads can use to work with you. This is a great way to give them an idea of what you can do together – with a customized roadmap!

CALL TO ACTION

One of the most overlooked aspects of free consultations is closing the call with a prompt or request. You may not like the "sales" aspect of the conversation because you don't want to be pushy.

Remember that your potential customer called because they have a need and are interested! If the consultation showed that you are an excellent match for the client's expressed needs, it is only natural to talk about the terms of working together.

Everyone has a different communication style. So, you may have to experiment with different ways of having this part of the conversation, so it sounds natural to your style of communication and personality. Map out a few alternatives and practice them.

CREATE A SCRIPT

To prepare yourself for the conversation and increase your chances to convert coaching leads to clients create a guide or a "script" that helps you organize your call. A script enables you to divide the time on the free consultation call and outline the options you offer.

A 'script' does not mean you have to read from the page, nor should you. You're not a robot. A script helps you to internalize the conversation so you can be in the moment, authentic, natural, and not caught up in hesitation and uncertainty because you don't know what to say or how to say it. This includes "the money conversation" where you will sooner or later have to answer the question about the price you charge.

Not preparing for this will make you sound even more awkward when you are caught off guard, perhaps rambling, or becoming nervous. Those behaviors reduce trust on the other side. Practice will help you to improve so you can convert coaching leads without sounding like a robot or a call center rep.

EXAMPLE OF A FREE CONSULTATION "SCRIPT"

Again, you don't *read* from the script. Internalize it so you are familiar with *the flow*, the typical questions, and the structure of services and pricing you offer so you are ready to provide this information when the time comes. You can use the example below as a starting point and modify it for your own needs. See it as a conversation script template, not a final solution. Make it your own and fit it to your style.

[CLIENT]: Hi, this is Emily. I am calling about the coaching. Is this a good time?

[COACH]: Hi Emily. So great to speak with you. What leads you to look for a coach in this area at this time?

[CLIENT]: Yes, thank you for asking. I have been spinning my wheels, I guess. [*Client goes on to explain their challenges...*]

[COACH]: That sounds challenging. [*Coach continues to reflect what s/he has heard and how coaching will address these challenges.*]

[COACH]: It sounds like the coaching will be a great fit to help you through those challenges so that you won't be spinning your wheels anymore. Do you agree?

[CLIENT]: Yes, I do.

[COACH]: Great. I do offer different options for coaching with me. Would you like to hear them?

[CLIENT]: Yes, that would be helpful.

[COACH]: Alright!

My first option is a _____ package for $_____. As option B, I offer _____ at the rate of _____. Which one of these do you prefer?

[CLIENT]: Is it possible to switch between these options?

[COACH]: Great question. Yes, that is possible at any time. Just give me at least a _____hour heads-up, and we'll switch you over to the other option. Which one do you prefer to start with?

[CLIENT]: I'd like to start with option A.

[COACH]: Wonderful. I'll have that set up for you today if you can share your email address with me.

[CLIENT]: Of course. Please use (email)@gmail.com.

[COACH]: And what card would you want to use for your payments?

[CLIENT]: Please use _____.

Ex. 1 - Free Consultation Script Example

What keeps your coaching business alive is the creation of leads and the ability to convert coaching leads to paying clients. Successful coaches are effective communicators who can relate well to others, and your conversion rate is proof of that.

In summary, to convert coaching leads to clients, you need to first find a way to attract coaching leads and get them interested in speaking with you. A great way to do that is by sharing your expertise through webinars, speaking events, podcasts, articles or blog posts, and lead magnets like white papers or checklists.

You will then have to provide a way for those interested in more information or in working with you to know where to go to speak with you. A landing page is often a way coaches achieve this. Another option is to simply set up an appointment booking page via Book Like A Boss, TidyCal, Calendly, or other providers.

You will also have to map out the flow of your free consultation call to prepare yourself for the conversation and increase your chances to convert coaching leads into customers. To do this, create a guide or a "script" that helps you organize your call. A script helps you to internalize the conversation so you can be in the moment, authentic, natural, and not caught up in hesitation and uncertainty because you don't know what to say or how to say it. Practice will help you to improve so you can build trust and convert coaching leads without sounding like a robot or a call center rep.

Tweak the sales conversion steps we have provided until this works for you.

Start Promoting Today

You may wonder where to begin when it comes to marketing your services. You could invest in ads, attend events, or directly contact people you suspect to fit your ideal target client.

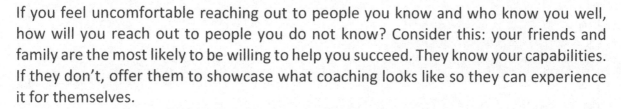

Knowing that most service business is won by referral, you should start with a different approach, or at least consider a mixed approach: Make a consolidated list of everyone you know, including friends, family, neighbors, previous coworkers, fellow gym-goers, and anyone you see regularly.

If you feel uncomfortable reaching out to people you know and who know you well, how will you reach out to people you do not know? Consider this: your friends and family are the most likely to be willing to help you succeed. They know your capabilities. If they don't, offer them to showcase what coaching looks like so they can experience it for themselves.

No, you are not asking your inner circle to become obnoxious salespeople, but you do want them to point to you if and when they have a conversation, say, with a coworker. When they hear of someone looking for a coach, they can point to you, that's all.

Before you communicate with any of them, have a clear and specific problem you can solve. You'll have to be able to speak to your network about *how* you can help other people. Think about what problems you solve through coaching. What needs of your client are you addressing? Make sure you communicate this in their language, not using typical coaching vocabulary. Think about the 2-3 key points you want them to remember when they walk away. How do you want them to introduce you to others?

Later in this book you will find a template to generate your brand statement. You can use that to prepare.

In addition, make sure you know how you want them to help you, whether that means introducing you to others, offering free coaching sessions, giving away your book or some other lead magnet, or something else.

Remember, people who already know you will be more willing to help if they see that you provide value. It's up to you to articulate it well.

Who can you reach out to today?

List five names of people who can help you get a speaking engagement, who would review your website or sales landing page, or who would let you coach them for free in exchange for valuable feedback?

1.

2.

3.

4.

5.

CREATING YOUR OWN VIDEOS

As a coach, get used to being on camera. It is an unspoken expectation these days that you have to be able to share your expertise with others. Of course, you can do this with whiteboard videos that don't show you live, but that is also proven to be less effective in establishing rapport with your audience than speaking into the camera.

Videos can be intimidating, but they don't have to be. You can start small, with a few simple steps once you have created a content plan with a list of topics you want to publish videos on:

Write out a clear, concise message or outline of the critical points for your video content. Tech-savviness is not an issue since most phones and laptop cameras work perfectly for video posts. Be sure the area is well lit, and the background is neutral without distractions or that chaotic stack of laundry drawing attention away from your message.

You can also ask for help writing a great pitch on a site like Fiverr for your first video so that it isn't lengthy and clearly communicates your message. Once you get the hang of the process, you can start practicing.

Another way to practice with a little helper is to use a teleprompter like BigVU. It's the same thing newscasters use when you watch the news. They read from a screen that tells them what to say.

Tools like Bigvu do the same for you. They can be loaded to your device, and you can see the text you had prepared on top of your video.

Practice a few times with a teleprompter and you will likely improve as you learn how to make your story more concise, catch your "ahs" and "uhms," and learn about what works best for you.

Even editing is easy today with simple online software that even kids use to look like video pros! **Try** Canva **or** InVideo **– two examples of free to low-cost tools** that come with loads of templates and design ideas and are quite fun to use.

Figure 19: BigVu example

Once you've published, continue to post *consistently* and let your audience know when the next video will be available for an extra boost of accountability. As you become more comfortable in front of the camera, you'll become better. Whatever you do, always preview your video before posting it online.

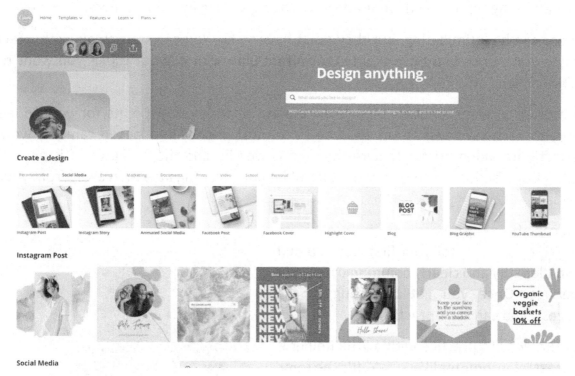

Figure 20: Canva screenshot

CREATING AN EMAIL LIST

I cannot stress this enough: **Build your email list early on, even if you only have three clients.** It helps you learn, while growing your audience little by little. If only one client forwards your email or refers you, you already have a multiplier.

You have the opportunity to show additional value to your subscribers, which can lead to additional or long-term business as people come to see you as an expert in your field.

Regardless of the list of potential or past clients who subscribe to your email list, regularly email them updates. Focus on a topic that addresses their questions, needs, pain points, and sparks their curiosity so your subscribers can look forward to each time they hear from you.

Once you have a decent list of subscribers, you won't need to place pricey ads to offer new services, or to sell your first book. You can simply share the good news with your subscribers, and there is a much higher chance they will respond because they already agreed to receive emails from you.

You can use a free or low-cost email tool that is surprisingly simple to use. Sendfox is the best software for their low price point in that area.

Using newsletter software will allow you to:

- Embed a form on your website to capture new subscribers

- Scan your website or blog for new content to automatically pull e.g., your latest blog post into an email that is ready to send to subscribers

- Get updates on how many people received your email (or, how many addresses are outdated/invalid)

- Get updates on how many people have opened or forwarded your email

- Reach your audience with additional offers or big updates

- Show your audience that you care about them (holiday greetings, anyone?)

The opportunities are nearly endless.

Where (Not) To Spend Your Advertising Budget

Are you tired of wasting your coaching ads budget? Perhaps you're the lucky one who hasn't wasted any budget yet, or you are the kind of entrepreneur who likes to plan well instead of experimenting. This article is for coaches who have a budget set aside for coaching ads and want to figure out the best way to reach their audience with a proper marketing strategy to reach their ideal client.

What Should You Consider For Coaching Ads

While everyone is jumping on YouTube ads, Instagram ads, and all the other trending platforms like TikTok, Snapchat, Twitter, etc., a lot of the budget for Facebook coaching ads and other coaching ads is wasted on "boosted posts" and other ads that were poorly planned and executed.

Before you invest in any marketing for coaching ads, invest in clarity on where your audience "hangs out" and which mediums would resonate the most with them.

For example, if you were targeting the elderly, certain digital platforms are unlikely to hit a large percentage of that demographic. You may get a few clients, but you want to maximize your results for every ad dollar you are spending and reach your ideal target client with your coaching ads.

Be Prepared To Include A Learning Budget

On the other hand, you have to be prepared to spend some "learning budget" on letting coaching ads run to gather data that will allow you to learn how your ad can be modified to be more effective.

Most ad platforms or social media ad services will provide a recommendation for how long you need to give an ad to see what works and what doesn't so you can fine-tune your campaign for maximum performance.

The key here is to make sure you are not overspending on your learning budget. If you do this, you won't be able to optimize your ads effectively. The goal should always be to find the right balance between the two budgets so that you can get the maximum return from each investment.

Popular Advertising Campaign Types

If you are new to paid advertising, it's important to know that there are different types of advertising campaigns available. These include:

Display Ads – These are the most common type of online advertising. They appear as banners, text links, images, videos, and popups.

Search Engine Optimization (SEO) – SEO refers to optimizing websites to rank higher in search engines such as Google. It includes things like keyword research, content creation, backlinks, and website optimization. Paid search ads like Google Ads also allow you to get ranked higher in search results without the more laborious work of organic SEO since Google Ads are paid placements.

Social Media Marketing (SMM) – SMM involves using social networks to promote products and brands. It also includes things like Facebook advertising, LinkedIn marketing, and influencer marketing.

Email Marketing – Email marketing allows companies to send targeted messages to customers. Companies use email marketing to build relationships with potential clients, increase brand awareness, and drive sales.

Mobile Advertising – Mobile advertising uses mobile devices such as smartphones and tablets to display advertisements.

Video Advertising – Video advertising is becoming increasingly popular because it offers businesses a great opportunity to connect with consumers as you share your expertise or entertain your audience to build rapport and become the go-to resource for specific topics.

Affiliate Marketing – In affiliate marketing, advertisers pay affiliates when someone clicks on their referral links or banners to purchase a product.

Referrals – Referral programs reward friends and family members for bringing new customers to your business.

Remarketing – Remarketing is like retargeting, except instead of showing ads to people who already visited your site, you show ads to people who visit sites that are similar to yours.

Content Marketing – This form of marketing focuses on creating valuable content that is useful to readers. This usually includes blog posts and video content.

Influencer Marketing – Influencer marketing is another way to market your business. Instead of paying celebrities directly, you partner with them to help spread your message.

ADS ARE NOT YOUR ULTIMATE SOLUTION TO A LACK OF CLIENTS

You may think that if you just spent enough money on advertising, then all of your problems would be solved. But this isn't true at all. A lot of coaches waste their marketing budget because of this assumption.

You still need to work effectively to attract clients. And even though you've invested a lot of time and money into advertising, you'll still need to constantly learn and adjust to the market and the data you track week to week to get the results you want. Advertising is not a one-and-done or a set-it-and-forget-it strategy. It takes consistent monitoring and improvement.

A WORD OF CAUTION REGARDING "RESULTS"

Hire a marketing professional who specializes in the ad category you are interested in and interview them to see if they understand the service you offer and the value you bring. Let them pitch their approach to you and compare a few experts before you hire someone.

Make sure you only sign up with a marketing consultant or with an advertising agency that can bring meaningful results. For example, merely promising views of your ad or clicks is not a meaningful result if you want to drive conversion.

To prepare yourself, create tangible business goals and explain to the marketing consultant or advertising agency you work with:

- what coaching clients you want to attract,

- what coaching services you want to promote,

- how advertising fits into your overall lead funnel,

- how long your marketing campaign will run initially,

- what advertising budget you have available,

- what results you expect from a marketing campaign,

- what support or advice you expect from your marketing expert,

- how the marketing agency will be held accountable and how often you expect updates.

Also, ensure that you speak to former or current clients who are coaching business owners like you to hear how they have been helped by the expert you plan to hire. A lot of money has been lost to "quick results" agencies who simply employ bots to generate the clicks you signed up for, leaving you without clients and with meaningless clicks you pay for.

Don't Neglect Traditional Paper Promotion

Depending on your niche, ready-to-share print collateral like a brochure may work better than digital coaching ads. Especially when your service is hyper-local and you can place flyers or posters with local partner businesses.

Building your Network (and Brand)

If you want to go fast, go alone.
If you want to go far, go together.
- African Proverb -

Start networking with fellow coaches early on. Community events, fairs, conferences, and professional association meetings are useful means to grow your network. These venues also serve as a way to build your reputation. You can offer free sample coaching or be a keynote speaker.

Networking with other coaches is also important to keep current on industry changes, exchange best practices, and stay motivated. Your business will take time to build, and you'll face a few challenges.

Other coaches who have started their own business will face similar challenges or have already gone before you and can provide advice.

Lastly, this can be an opportunity to partner with other businesses. You could partner with another coach, or you might find other partners who complement your services and vice versa. For example, career coaches can partner with local government agencies who offer free career services to their local citizens. As a coach, you will make a lot of connections here that can become clients down the road. Wellness coaches may partner with businesses adjacent to their offer. This could give you the opportunity to get referrals or to generate additional income by creating a mutual agreement to cross-promote services.

FINDING AND
COACHING CLIENTS

S. Finding and Coaching Clients

You can find clients in many places: on social platforms like LinkedIn or Facebook, in real life meetings like local networking events, or though speaking engagements, and industry events. But you can also "be found" by clients via search engines or via specific coaching directories.

Being found via search engines is a big topic that we are not going to cover in detail in this segment. We will just say for now that it requires clarity on who you cater to, what problem you solve, what your audience wants to know about and generating consistent – and well-coordinated – content around it to rank high in search results. You also have the option to pay for your placement in e.g., Google search results and we recommend you work with an industry expert to do so.

As a new coach, you can be found by clients by using coaching directories and lead marketplaces. The latter is a place where you pay for leads. The former is usually costing you a monthly or annual fee for being listed and visible in the directory.

Most coaches do have a few clients in the beginning, then often experience a lag. That's okay! This can be seasonal or due to inconsistencies in your approach.

Keep reflecting on what you learn has worked and what needs improvement. As you learn and grow, so will your business. Keep at it.

Joining a networking group of peer coaches will help you learn with and from others and keep you motivated. You can join our Business Clinic to systematically work on building your business while simultaneously networking with your peers.

Keep reaching out and follow up with any undecided potential clients. If persistently keep following up until they are ready for change, they will choose you because you've kept in touch. Of course, this takes deliberate and disciplined effort on your part to end each undecided call with a confident response that you'll be in touch.

For printable versions of the worksheets in this part of the book, go to Coachilly.com/coaching-startup-worksheets and use password "start" to access the site.

DEFINE YOUR COACHING NICHE IN 6 STEPS

Most people get so excited about starting a business that the first thing they do is work on a business name and logo. Don't do that. You have to have some fundamentals covered before you proceed to that part. It'll be worthwhile, I promise.

If you create a business name, register your business, and design a logo before laying a solid foundation, you may find yourself abandoning your business or rebranding in a few months. Believe me, that's a waste of your resources. It's time-consuming and unnecessary.

Some coaches have very defined niches, meaning they can articulate very clearly to whom they are catering. Others have more difficulties narrowing down their niches.

In essence, a niche is a very defined market segment that you decide to serve. It sets clear boundaries of who you want to primarily target. That said, this doesn't mean you won't get clients outside of that target, but you'll send a clear message to your target group that tells them that they are the customers on whom you focus your business. It makes them feel understood and builds trust that you can help them since you address their challenges head on.

Some entrepreneurs have difficulties setting such boundaries and view a niche as constricting their revenue opportunities. In reality, trying to target too many markets, or types of clients, at once can backfire:

Instead of reaching everyone by trying to be everything to everyone, an unfocused business is often reaching no one.

The reason these businesses are not well-received is because their message isn't clearly targeting their audience - in other words, audiences don't see their unique needs being addressed.

You may ask now, "Can't you serve more than one customer?" Yes, it's possible, but you usually don't start like that, and if you do, you would still identify the overlaps in your client segments, so your messaging is clear.

EXAMPLE OF NICHE MARKETS

A niche sounds tiny, but make no mistake, a niche can be of almost any size and growth potential. An example of a niche can be found in every industry. For example, there used to be a website called Diapers.com focused on diapers. The need they identified: affordable diapers online. The need for affordable diapers delivered to the home was so great, in fact, that the company grew and was later sold to Amazon.com for a whopping $545 million.

Defining a niche can mean addressing a specific geography, e.g., a medical concierge service targeting only one city or state. You can also use demographic segmentation such as providing tailor-made business clothes to women.

You know you have been part of a niche market whenever you were attracted to buy from a company *who specialized on the exact need you had*. For me, this had been a company focused on providing single-pack nutrition for frequent travelers. It addressed my need perfectly by providing individually packed, high-quality products such as protein, or my source of healthy fruits and veggies in powder or pill-packs, so I would not lack in nutrients while traveling.

To find your niche, think of the overlap between you and the world. The image below illustrates this by putting you on one side and the world on the other. You have a passion (your WHY) and a set of skills and experience to offer in form of products and services (your HOW).

The world, on the other hand, has needs and interests that they are willing to pay for (that's where their needs are assigned a value, called budget). When they match, you have a market. How big the market is must be determined by you.

Is it enough to know there is a market? No. The size of the market matters. External factors matter, such as legal requirements, other companies in that market, big trends changing the market, and so forth. There are volumes of books written on how markets can be predicted, how they change, how to analyze them, why companies fail, etc.

Once you have narrowed down a niche, you will need to continue following industry news, observing the market, and growing your knowledge further to refine your approach.

After the overall market niche is identified – represented by the red square in the middle – you proceed to narrow down your Unique Selling Proposition (USP). A USP is a marketing term and describes what sets you, your business, and your products and services truly apart from others.

Let's view the square representing the niche market as your diamond in the rough. Your USP is your polished diamond, desirable to those you serve!

To get to the USP, you need to identify in a few more steps what can truly set you apart in the niche market you have just zeroed-in on:

(1) Take a look at your competitors. Your competitors already cover the needs in the niche market. Sometimes people say, "I don't have competitors." That's because they haven't identified them yet.

Competitors do not always compete directly. They can cover the needs of your clients in a completely different way and in a different industry. Your question to ask is: How are my target clients currently satisfying their needs in this area?

(2) Next, you will look at the overall market and narrow down the target group. Who among this group is not sufficiently helped? Who can you help the most because of your unique makeup of passion, talent, solutions, and experience? This demographic needs to be described. You will get a chance to do this later in the workbook section of this book.

(3) Lastly, identify gaps in the services offered. This is about identifying what needs are still unaddressed, or poorly addressed, by existing solutions.

The result is your defendable USP. Defendable, because everyone can say they are unique or better than others. That's not tangible or believable until you can defend it with facts. With this exercise, you can defend it, although you won't need to do so.

Your USP will help you to articulate your value because you have just done the legwork of finding out how you can be the perfect match for your target group in your niche market.

When you articulate what you can do for your target group, you have their attention. Your USP will resonate with them. They will feel heard and that brings you trust. Trust is GOLD in sales terms! We buy from those we trust to deliver what we need. Only then do we part with money.

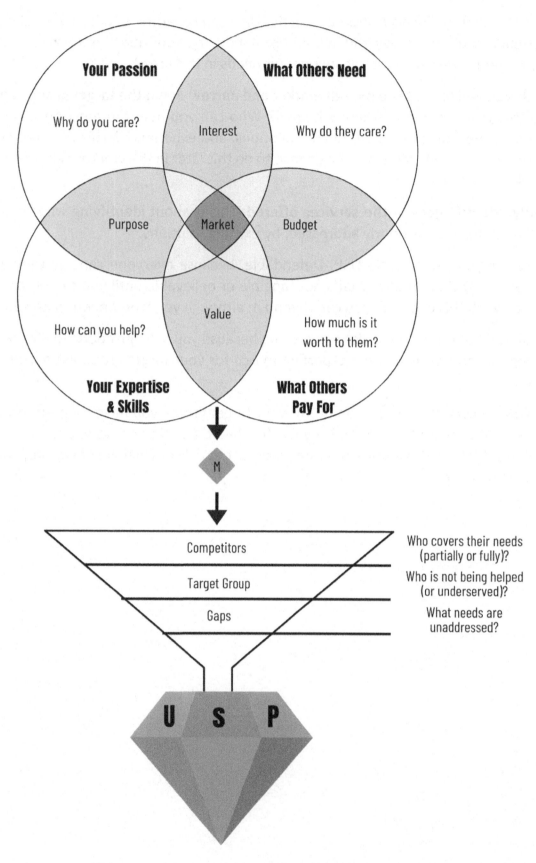

Figure 21 Finding Your Niche and USP

What's Your Niche?

Keeping the previous graphic in mind, let's think practically through the services or products you can offer: What are the customer challenges you can solve with services and products?

Who needs these services the most?

Who is your target group? Are they men or women? Frequent travelers? Does age matter? Education? Career level? Family status? Location? Etc.

Who else is offering similar products or services?

Remember the earlier discussion on looking for competitors by asking, "How does my target group currently satisfy their needs?"

What part of the market is not covered? What are other customer needs that you can cover (profitably) with products and services?

What gaps did you discover?

What is not done well by the current providers (setting an expectation or industry standard that clients expect now)?

o
o
o
o
o
o
o
o
o

HOW BIG IS YOUR NICHE?

For example, demographic + industry - in the above example, you would look up the industry for specialty nutrition plus the number of frequent travelers or female business travelers depending on your focus to start sizing your market.

o
o
o
o
o
o
o
o
o
o

Now, describe your niche in one sentence with this template. Don't get caught up with your business name yet.

My business provides _____ to
(product/service)
_____ in _____ who
(target group)   (market segment or location)
need _____ and/or
(specific customer challenge, need)
_____ to _____.
(challenge/need #2)   (overall need)

For example:

My business provides individually packaged protein packs **to** female business travelers **in** the U.S. **who need** healthy nutrition **and/or** easy-to-combine solutions **to** suit their unique nutritional needs on-the-go.

You can use this going forward as you introduce your business or what you do for others. Don't get too attached to it yet. This statement may change as you get feedback from the market and fine tune your business, but it is good to have clarity on who you serve and what you do as a means of introducing yourself with confidence.

WHO ARE YOUR BUYER PERSONAS?

What's a buyer persona? Think of this as giving your target customer(s) a name and specific characteristics.

To stick with the travel nutrition example, you may have two different female travelers – one is Katie. Katie is focused on lean, healthy nutrition and does not want to miss out on her greens. She wants to stay energized and boost her immune system as she sleeps in hotels and has limited choices with her heavy travel schedule.

The second buyer persona is Leela. Leela is also a frequent traveler. Her focus is on nutrition that supports a very active lifestyle. Leela is an avid runner and needs her travel nutrition to support her pre- and post-workout needs.

These are summarized examples for buyer personas. The better you describe your buyer persona, the more specific you get, and the better you can use targeting in your content and ads to reach this audience. A little investment of time in this area will go a long way.

To define your persona(s), define key items below using the template. You can do this here or you can use the excellent, simple, and fun (yes, fun!) online Buyer Persona Creation tool provided by HubSpot (it's free!). It's B2B focused (business-to-business), but you can modify it for your own needs.

Keep these persona profiles handy. You will need them when you create your website, your sales landing pages, and each time you write blog posts of interest to your audience, create ads to reach this audience, and so on.

Using the template below, describe your target customer (buyer persona).

Give him/her a name you can remember. This is the (type of) person you will be speaking to and doing work for!

1. Describe the buyer persona's demographic:

   a. Age

   b. Income

   c. Location

   d. Level of education

   e. Industry

   f. Language

2. What's the *best* way to reach them? (Phone, Email, Social Media, etc.)

3. What are their goals?

4. What are their challenges?

5. How do they solve these challenges currently?

6. Where do they find solutions for these goals and challenges (sources)?

For example, they may follow health and wellness blogs, Facebook groups, follow experts on social media, or subscribe to magazines or attend events.

CUSTOMER (BUYER) PERSONA TEMPLATE

1. Name: _____

2. Demographics:

   a. Age: _____

   b. Income: _____

   c. Location: _____

   d. Education: _____

   e. Industry: _____

   f. Language: _____

   g. Other: _____

3. Preferred communication: _____

4. Goals: _____

5. Challenges: _____

6. Current solutions: _____

WHAT CAN YOU OFFER YOUR CUSTOMERS (THAT THEY'LL PAY FOR)?

If you read this headline thinking, "Duh, I will offer coaching!" think again. What will customers pay for? A coaching session? Think again.

Customers pay for perceived *value*. You need to be able to articulate that in a tangible way. What will the coaching *do* for the person? What changes, what outcomes can be expected? In addition, you may want to ask yourself what complementary services you could offer that would further enhance your clients' lives. Is it a book, a course, or worksheets?

Take some time to search for a coach in any field and you will find endless options to provide helpful services and products to clients that complement your coaching.

Even for your coaching services, think about how you will present them. After you have defined the value you bring through tangible benefits, think through the options you will provide and the pricing. Will you offer single sessions or exclusively offer session-packages? How will you price them? Does a subscription make sense? What is common in your niche market?

Let's do some research. Put yourself into the shoes of a customer. Pick a niche that does not resemble yours for this exercise. Google "find a coach" and add the topic you're interested in.

You could search "find an Emotional Intelligence coach in Denver" and go through the results. Some will be listed on marketplaces for the service industry or specific coaching platforms like LifeCoachHub or Coaching.com.

Take notes on what you learn about offerings, prices, communicated value, etc. Which of these attract you and why? What builds your trust in such a way that the coach can help in that area?

Take these learnings to ideate your service offering. Create your services and offer them on your website, or on these marketplaces. Don't worry, you will likely refine your offerings over time as you receive feedback from your audience.

COME UP WITH A GREAT NAME FOR YOUR BUSINESS

Now the fun part! Like most people, you have been waiting for this. Many coaches romanticize this part together with working on a logo and business cards. But having clarity about the value you'll bring will make this step not only easier, but will also help you to create a name that will endure doubts, challenges, and even changes you will make to your business model. Make no mistake, it is not an endeavor to take lightly. You'll stick with your business name for a long time. The business name you'll pick will also have to meet a few standards you should consider:

o It must resonate with your audience.

o It must be memorable. It should be distinct, not to be confused with other businesses or associated with a product or industry different than yours.

o It must be available (not taken by other businesses or already registered as a web domain).

o It should be easy to pronounce and spell. Spelling errors may lead your audience to a different company.

To come up with business names can be a science project. To simplify, I recommend you use tools like Namelix to come up with ideas. This website provides a unique tool that creates not only business name suggestions, but also logo options that often match the tone of your brand name. Make sure you also check the results against domain name availability, using tools like HostArmada or NameCheap. You can use NorthWest Registered Agent to also check that the matching business name is available.

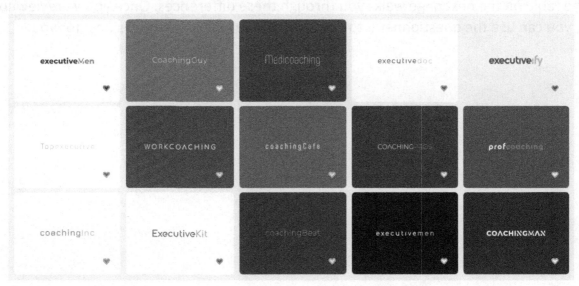

Figure 22 - Namelix examples

Come up with at least thirty (30) names. Put the list aside for a day and return to it the next day to review. Narrow the list down to twenty names for a first survey or select five names per your preference and send it to your personal network for feedback. I recommend using SurveyMonkey (free) or Google Forms (free) to create a simple survey. Send them a note asking to help you out. Most "wantrepreneurs" (want-to-be entrepreneurs) report that they usually get a high response rate from their personal and professional network.

Here is an example of a survey you can copy and modify for your purposes: Brand Name Survey I (requires that you have a Google account and are logged in). Use the feedback from your network to refine the name until you are confident about the result.

WHAT TYPE OF BUSINESS WILL YOURS BE?

What type of business should you register? An LLC? An Inc? Do you need any at all? What are the differences?

Many have asked the same question, which is why I have put together a decision guide to look at a few types of businesses and their differences, implications, as well as pros and cons.

Some specifics can change by state and at any time as local laws change. You can use the linked list of states to find your state rules in Nolo's guide: "Small Business License Requirements: A 50-State Guide" and start the process and see if anything has changed.

The table on the next page walks you through these differences. Once you've reviewed it, you can use the questionnaire to help you decide which solution is best for you.

	Sole Proprietorship	LLC	C-Corporation	S-Corporation
Overview	Sole Proprietorship is the simplest business structure, involving one individual as the owner running the business. Its appeal is the simplicity of filing income and expenses via one's individual tax return, and reporting profit and loss via Schedule C, which is amended to your form 1040. Sole Proprietorship, however, does not protect your personal assets.	An LLC offers the benefits of incorporation and pass-through taxation and is usually used for small businesses who want to protect their personal assets. This is attractive to individuals who want the "best of both worlds" - a hybrid between Sole Proprietorship and Corporation.	A C-Corporation[1] is a standard corporation and a separate legal entity owned by its shareholders and taxed separately from its owners. This form of business limits each owner's (shareholder's) personal liability to their investments in the company.	An S-Corporation[2] is similar to a C-Corporation with the exception that it is usually used for small business and elected special tax status with the IRS, which allows the owner to "pass through" business losses via their individual tax returns.
Personal liability	Unlimited liability with personal assets (for details, see Nolo's page on business formation for Sole Proprietors and click on your state).	Limited liability, not affecting personal assets - with exceptions (for details, see Nolo's page on business formation and click on your state).	Company is liable, personal assets are protected - with exceptions (for details, see Nolo's page on business formation for Corporations).	Company is liable, personal assets are protected - with exceptions (for details, see Nolo's page on business formation for S-Corporations).

---

[1] A C corporation or C Corp (named for being in subchapter "C" of the Internal Revenue code) is an independent legal entity owned by its shareholders. A C corporation's profit is taxed twice—as business income at the entity level and the shareholder level when distributed as dividends or realized as capital gains. (via Taxfoundation.org)

[2] An S corporation is a business entity which elects to pass business income and losses through to its shareholders. The shareholders are then responsible for paying individual income taxes on this income. (via Taxfoundation.org)

	Sole Proprietorship	LLC	C-Corporation	S-Corporation
Ownership	One person, the owner is the sole proprietor.	At least two people (no maximum).	No restriction to the number of shareholders.	Can have a maximum of 100 shareholders.
Business Continuation	Dissolves when the owner deceases or retires.	Unless the operating agreement (OA) states otherwise, the company dissolves when a member leaves the LLC. This can be prevented in the OA by including "buy-sell" or a buyout option with guidelines in the case of death or retirement of a member or another reason for leaving the LLC to be able to continue business.	Perpetual, meaning the company continues to exist even when a partner leaves the organization.	Perpetual, meaning the company continues to exist even when a partner leaves the organization.

	Sole Proprietorship	LLC	C-Corporation	S-Corporation
Administrative Overhead	Minimal.	Manageable.	Considerable. Must follow requirements for corporate record-keeping, filing of forms every year, and pay corporate filing fees.	Considerable. Must follow requirements for corporate record-keeping, filing of forms every year, and pay corporate filing fees.
Tax implication	• Filed with personal income tax (just another source of income) • Pass-through tax treatment [3]	• Not recognized as separate tax entity by IRS • Paid via personal income tax • Payment of self-employment taxes and Social Security	• Taxed as a separate entity (filed separately, not with personal income taxes) • Double taxation (see "cons" below)	• No tax on company profits possible • Taxes paid on the owner's (also a shareholder who works for the company) salary • Pass-through tax treatment

---

[3] "When a pass-through business earns profits, it does not directly send a portion of the profits to the Internal Revenue Service (IRS). Instead, the profit is "passed through" the business and onto the tax returns of the business owners. The owners are then responsible for paying the tax to the IRS. That means that pass-through businesses pay individual income taxes, not corporate income taxes." (via Taxfoundation.org)

	Sole Proprietorship	LLC	C-Corporation	S-Corporation
Minimum requirements	• License or permit • Register business with local government	• Choose a (unique, distinct) business name which includes "LLC" in the name without restricted words (e.g., "bank") • File articles of organization • create operating agreement • Obtain licenses and permits • Follow federal and state regulations for employers • (selected states) announce/ publish business in local newspaper	• Election of a board of directors by shareholders required • Regular meetings for both directors and shareholders have to be scheduled • Board and shareholder meetings have to be recorded in meeting minutes • Compliance with any state or local business licensing requirements (e.g., retaining legal counsel, which can be costly) • Extensive administrative requirements: • File articles of incorporation with the state secretary • Create and record a set of bylaws (often requires costly legal services) • Must use the accrual method for accounting	• See C-Corporation • Owners are shareholders and required to pay themselves a salary that matches industry salaries for similar jobs • Each shareholder must be a U.S. citizen or resident (not a requirement for C-Corporations) • Shareholders cannot deduct corporate losses beyond their stock basis or company investment • Fringe benefits to employee shareholders who own over 2% of the corporation cannot be deducted.

	Sole Proprietorship	LLC	C-Corporation	S-Corporation
Who should consider it	• Businesses operated by one individual (e.g., freelancers, consultants, coaches) • Low business risk (since the owner is personally liable)	• Business with higher risk of affecting personal assets • Businesses with more than one employee (although many single-employee LLCs exist) • Startups expecting losses for at least two years that they want to pass through to you on your individual tax return • Preference for flexibility of accounting methods (accrual vs. cash) • Minimize requirements for strict ongoing formalities (as the C-Corporation has)	• Businesses who plan to raise money from the public or seek to have investors. • Fringe benefits are fully deductible • Companies who plan to offer their employees stock options and similar incentives. • Companies who want flexible profit sharing among owners. • Businesses who plan to provide substantial fringe benefits and stock options to their employees.	• Companies without inventory can use the (simpler) cash accounting method instead of the accrual method. • Owners are allowed to "pass through" business losses on individual tax returns • Taxable gain at the point of selling your business can be less than a regular corporation • Shareholders are not subject to self-employment taxes as LLC owners are.

	Sole Proprietorship	LLC	C-Corporation	S-Corporation
Pros	• Easy to set up, lower cost to form • Low administrative maintenance / convenience • Easy to dissolve • Easy tax filing (with personal income tax rather than separate filing for the business)	• Limited liability • Low start-up costs • Less paperwork than S-corporation • No separate corporate return required (filed with personal tax return) • No double-taxation • No need for strict, ongoing formalities as the C-/or S-Corporation with bylaws, director or shareholder meetings, etc.	• Does not affect individual assets • Business continuity - does not dissolve like the LLC when an owner leaves or goes bankrupt • Can retain some of its profits, without the owner paying tax on them • Ability to raise money by selling stock to raise funds • Lower risk of IRS tax audits due to regular, strict reporting requirements.	• Special status as "Subchapter" allows to avoid filing corporate returns (just one tax return to file - your personal one) • Owners/ shareholders pay income tax on salary, but may or may not owe any taxes on the company's profits • Life goes on even if an owner leaves the company (opposite to LLCs) • Can have up to 100 shareholders • No double-taxation as the C-corporation has

	Sole Proprietorship	LLC	C-Corporation	S-Corporation

Cons	• personal liability
	
	• self-employment tax on 100% of the income
	
	• public perception or standing among potential partners and banks (often getting funding only once you're incorporated)
	
	• Mixing personal and business expenses can be a challenge, requiring a lot of self-discipline
		• Self-employment taxes, Medicare and Social Security tax applied to profits.
		
		• Requirement to dissolve if a member (owner) leaves an LLC
		
		• Potential disruption of business if an owner decides to leave or goes bankrupt - the LLC automatically dissolves. Remaining owners would have to register a company / file for incorporation again.
		
		• Some states (Massachusetts or DC) require more than one person to form an LLC - check the Nolo guide referenced above to see latest rules for your state.
			• Double taxation:
			
			  ○ as the corporation itself
			
			  ○ taxing of shareholder's dividends on individual tax returns
			
			• Double taxation can be avoided if you pay shareholders (including yourself) in form of a salary if it is considered reasonable compensation by the IRS.
			
			• Requires shareholder meetings
			
			• Requires director meetings
			
			• Strict rules for ongoing formalities such as bylaws, meeting records, etc.
			
			• High administrative efforts to keep accounting and tax records
			
			• High(er) cost
				• See C-Corporation
				
				• Administrative requirements from federal, state and local governments as also required of C-Corporations
				
				• Higher cost of maintaining (e.g., legal fees, administrative requirements)
				
				• Higher IRS tax audit rate due to the informational tax return filing.

Questionnaire		Path / Options			
	Answer	Sole Proprietor	LLC	S-Corporation	C-Corporation
Are you starting a business by yourself?	Yes	x	x	x	
Are you starting a business by yourself?	No				x
Future needs: Do you plan to raise funds from investors?	Yes				x
Future needs: Do you plan to raise funds from investors?	No	x	x	x	
Is your business of low risk and are you OK with being personally liable with your personal assets?	Yes	x			
Is your business of low risk and are you OK with being personally liable with your personal assets?	No		x	x	x
Do you plan to hand the business over to the next generation or a member of your company in the future?	Yes		x	?	x
Do you plan to hand the business over to the next generation or a member of your company in the future?	No	x			
Do you have the capacity and/or knowledge or resources to deal with the administrative overhead required by a corporation?	No	x	x		
Do you have the capacity and/or knowledge or resources to deal with the administrative overhead required by a corporation?	Yes			x	x

	Answer	Sole Proprietor	LLC	S-Corporation	C-Corporation
If you plan to have shareholders - are you OK to be limited to a maximum of 100 shareholders?	Yes			x	
If you plan to have shareholders - are you OK to be limited to a maximum of 100 shareholders?	No				x
Do you expect for your company to make losses over the next two years that you wish to pass through your individual tax return to lower your taxable income?	Yes		x	x	
Do you expect for your company to make losses over the next two years that you wish to pass through your individual tax return to lower your taxable income?	No	x			s
Is your business a freelance type of business (consulting, legal advice, coaching)?	Yes	x	x		
Is your business a freelance type of business (consulting, legal advice, coaching)?	No			x	x
If you plan to register as a Corporation: is your company without inventory?	Yes			x	
If you plan to register as a Corporation: is your company without inventory?	No				x
Do you plan to sell the company mid-term?	Yes			x	x
Do you plan to sell the company mid-term?	No	x	x		
Are you willing to pay self-employment tax?	Yes	(via your personal tax return)	x		
Are you willing to pay self-employment tax?	No			x	x
Are you OK with double taxation (the company itself and shareholder dividends)?	Yes				x
Are you OK with double taxation (the company itself and shareholder dividends)?	No	x	x	x	

SETTING UP YOUR COACHING SYSTEM

In Part III, where you found resources for your coaching business, we saw the need to establish a system and an organization around it to *operationalize* coaching. That means, you need to define the process and the steps you will need to repeat each time you talk to a lead, sign a new coaching contract, onboard a customer, start a coaching session, and so forth.

This process description is extremely important for you if you do not want to lose your sanity (and your customers) as your business begins to grow. It will also become important when you begin to hire assistance or other coaches who need to follow your process to provide a consistent experience to your clients.

As soon as you sign more than a handful of clients, you will have added complexity as you need to remember details for multiple people. All of this is happening while you also get busy building your brand on social media and create posts, update your website, and maintain your books (accounting) to be up to date when taxes are due, etc.

To stay on top of all of the items you are responsible for on your own until you can afford to hire others to help you, I recommend you document what you do and how you do it. We're not overcomplicating this exercise. The purpose of your coaching system is to help you run your business, so your customers are led through their lifecycle with you as smoothly as possible and you are able to work efficiently without frantically searching for information when you urgently need it.

At a high level, describe the process your customer goes through from the time they hear about you and become a customer, until they stop working with you. What process do you guide them through? You need to establish consistency – the same procedure, every time. The better you define this, the more efficient you will be able to handle the process without manual and time-consuming adjustments. This will also help you to onboard an employee down the line should you be able to hire one. You can use this as the "manual" for how to work with your customers.

You can use a Word document with an inserted table to do this. I recommend this format, because it is easier for most people to add multiple lines for the same field as you will do in this exercise.

Add the customer touchpoint or stage in the journey in column A. In column B, add the procedure. In column C, list the tools and templates you use to do this. In column D, you can list links to the places where those tools and templates reside.

Stage	Procedure (steps)	Tools & Templates	Location
Lead / Interest	1. Self-schedules phone consultation 2. Automatic email confirmation 3. Automatic creation of record in CRM 4. Automatic appointment on calendar	1. Acuity Scheduling 2. Acuity Scheduling 3. HubSpot 4. Google Calendar	1. Link 2. Link 3. Link 4. Link
Purchase / Booking	1. Set up in coaching system 2. Send welcome invitation and contract 3. ...	1. Delenta 2. Delenta	1. Link 2. Link

Now you have a simple, documented process that is organized and clearly shows what happens when and where, who's involved, and what is used.

I recommend another list to stay organized early on in your business: the services you use. Before you know it, you will use more than a handful. Many of them will be free for small businesses, while some will cost a small monthly fee. As time goes by, you find yourself with a bouquet of software and services that will need to be maintained (e.g., updating your address).

To get this list of services and software started, you can use a simple spreadsheet. There are different ways to keep track of your system. For simplicity, let's list your tools and services for the functional business areas (finance, sales, coaching operations, marketing, etc.). The image below shows an example and was created using Airtable. It is easy to sort through your data; for example, I have grouped them by business function for this example.

You see, you may end up using several tools for marketing. Some may overlap with others. You can use this also to track your expenses by adding a column for the monthly, annual, or one-time fees you paid to use some of these providers.

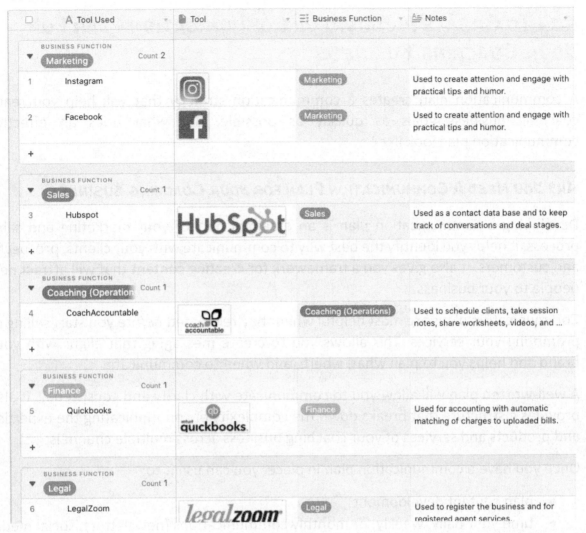

Figure 23: Airtable example

How To Create A Powerful Communication Plan For Your Coaching Business

A communication plan creates a communication strategy that will help you reach coaching business goals as quickly as possible. But what does an effective communication plan look like?

Why You Need A Communication Plan for your Coaching Business

Developing a communication plan is an essential part of your marketing and sales process. It helps you identify the best way to communicate with your clients, prospects, and customers. It also gives you a framework for creating content that will attract new people to your business.

Communication plans are most helpful when they're created *before* you start selling or promoting your services. This allows you to create messaging that aligns with your brand and helps you to plan what, where, and when to communicate.

A well-written plan will allow you to communicate with clarity and consistency. It also provides a structure that breaks down the complexity of communicating the expertise and products and services of your coaching business across multiple channels.

Once you have a communication plan in place, you can use it to:

- plan content development
- time your daily, weekly, or monthly communications (newsletters, social media posts, etc.)
- fine-tune your activities if you see what is or is not working well
- create synergies to avoid the overproduction of content
- plan ahead of launches to create "buzz" in anticipation of a newly launched product or even to plan your business launch announcement.

What A Communication Plan for a Coaching Business Needs

What a good communication plan needs depends on who you're targeting and how much time you want to spend developing your message. If you're looking to sell more coaching packages, then you'll need to focus on creating a clear value proposition that makes it easy for potential buyers to understand why they should buy from you.

If you're planning to build a mailing list of subscribers, then you'll need a different approach than if you're trying to get leads through cold calling. The same goes for social media. If you're hoping to grow your email list by posting links to blog articles, then you'll need something else entirely.

The following sections outline some key components of a good communications plan.

1. Identify Your Target Audience

Who do you want to talk to? Who do you want to hear from? What do they care about? How do they prefer to receive information?

2. Define Your Message

What's your main point? Why should someone buy from you? What problem are you solving? What benefits will they gain?

3. Choose Your Communication Channels

Which platforms will you use to deliver your message? Will you post regularly or just occasionally? Which marketing channels will you employ? When?

4. Develop Content

What kind of content will you share? Blog posts? Videos? Infographics? Articles? Podcasts? Emails? Social media updates? Where will your marketing materials be stored?

5. Measure Results

How will you measure success? Are there any metrics you can track? Do you need to set up a system to keep track of results?

6. Plan Improvements

As you learn more about your audience and your goals, you may find that you need to adjust your strategy. You might decide to change your tone, frequency, or medium. Or maybe you realize that one channel isn't working as well as another.

7. Evaluate And Revise

As you continue to develop your plan, you'll be able to evaluate whether it's effective and refine it accordingly.

You've created a well-thought-out plan. Now use your plan to execute it and announce your upcoming launch – whether your business launch or your next product launch.

HOW TO USE YOUR COMMUNICATION PLAN IN YOUR DAILY COACHING BUSINESS ACTIVITIES

You don't necessarily need to write out an entire plan before you start your marketing activities. Instead, you can make adjustments along the way based on what you observe. Here are some ideas for how you could use your communication plan in your day-to-day activities:

Write a short summary of your weekly plan at the beginning of each week so you know where you stand. This helps you stay focused on what you're doing and prevents you from getting distracted by other things.

Create a document or use a project management tool or a professional content planner to keep track of your activities. For example, if your communication plan indicates that you are blogging weekly and posting on Instagram daily, you need a planner to keep track of it. You could use a spreadsheet to do it as well if that works for you.

However, spreadsheets often make it hard to connect to other apps and to track multiple formats well. This is where great marketing planners or content planning tools come in handy. Take a look at CoSchedule, Missinglettr, Publr, or even Canva's built-in scheduling tool and see what works for you.

Lastly, check out some free communication plan templates from Hubspot to start your planning with proven methods. This way, you do not need to wonder about how to write a communication plan from scratch.

Some coaches dread the work of performing regular marketing activities just to generate coaching leads. It's understandable – you want to spend time coaching clients! You have several options to create leads – they range in effort and effectiveness.

We've decided – just for this article – to exclude funnels, social media and email outreach, events, and ads. Instead, we are focusing exclusively on directory-style platforms that put you in front of thousands, in some cases millions of leads. These directories are also called marketplaces and we found five marketplaces that we think are a great fit to get coaching leads.

KEY DIFFERENCES IN HOW YOU PAY FOR COACHING LEADS

Each lead platform has its own business model. The main differences in the pricing model are

- Paying for membership – usually annually
- Paying a fixed fee per lead
- Paying a percentage per converted lead
- A combination of the above

EXAMPLES OF PAGES TO GET COACHING LEADS:

NOOMII

Noomii focuses specifically on coaching leads. This coaching directory has been around for many years and helps you to create a great coaching profile.

If you sign up with Noomi, you will be offered to schedule a call to record an audio interview with a Noomii employee. This is entirely optional but very beneficial as this recording gives you the opportunity to talk about your business and who you're helping.

Look around Noomii's directory and listen to a few recordings from other coaches to get ideas.

Noomi's Fee Structure

Noomii charges an annual fee. Coaching leads who contact you directly via your profile are yours to keep without extra fees.

If you decide to apply to be matched to leads in their daily updated leads list, be prepared to pay 30% of your contract value for these types of leads.

THUMBTACK

Thumbtack focuses on leads in many categories, including coaching. This is one of the largest lead generation platforms with over 10 million users.

You have a range of tools available on your profile to make your business stand out. Thumbtack provides tips on how to improve your profile and you will see a "completion score" as well. For example, profiles with videos or images get more coaching leads.

Thumbtack's Fee Structure

You set your budget every week. If you do not change it, it remains the same. The beauty here is that you can change your budget based on your business needs. If you have a lot of clients, you can dial your budget down or turn it off.

Fees for leads differ based on your rates and on the type of service. Thumbtack provides previews for the cost per lead so you're not getting caught by surprise.

The great thing about Thumbtack is, you pay only once for the lead without any fees for joining the platform or any contingency fees as share of revenue.

LIFECOACHHUB

LifeCoachHub focuses on providing you with coaching leads.

LifeCoachHub's Fee Structure

Joining their directory to get listed as a coach is entirely free. If you want to get a "featured listing" that shows up on top of your coaching category when a lead looks for a coach in your field, you will have to join a priced plan. At the time of writing this article, the fee for additional features, including a featured directory listing, is $37 per month.

COACHING.COM

Coaching.com is a somewhat "new kid on the block". Somewhat, because it's not entirely new. The names CoachLogix and WBECS may sound familiar to you if you've been a coach for a while. In 2022, Coaching.com acquired WBECS after the coaching software platform CoachLogix had rebranded itself to Coaching.com.

Today, Coaching.com is a 3-in-1 solution as we explained in our detailed review of this online coaching platform (cloud software). Coaching.com provides:

A coaching marketplace (a profile listing in their directory, which matches coaching leads with coaches)

An online coaching platform (coaching software to run your coaching operations)

Coaching education via WBECS. WBECS offers a year-long online summit with high-profile speakers from across the globe. Their education content is approved for CCEs (Continuing Coach Education Credits) by the ICF (International Coach Federation). Coaches need these to accrue learning hours toward their coaching certification.

The coaching marketplace is having extremely high potential to get your coaching business found online because it uses the most obvious domain name one would google when searching for a coach. What's better than "coaching.com"?

Coaching.com's Fee Structure

Join their directory for free and get a basic online coaching platform account (coaching software) included.

For clients who find you through their marketplace, you'd pay between 25% if you have a free account.

For coaches choosing to sign up for premium tiers, the commission fee goes down to 20% or 15%.

Attention: regardless of this commission fee, coaches pay between 1-5% for payments collected through the platform, after other fees for payment processors (e.g., Stripe) are paid.

LinkedIn Services

LinkedIn Services is part of the popular LinkedIn social networking platform. This is the largest business network with a whopping 800 million members worldwide and growing!

You can set up your profile at no cost, but to get leads, you will have to join their paid service. The great advantage for coaches in the business, leadership, executive, and career coaching niches find their entire target audience conveniently in one place.

Many coaches resort to creating endless connection requests with insincere messaging that is often perceived as spam. Instead, you can either change your strategy to stand out from other coaches who employ sleazy strategies or choose a different avenue that responds directly to those who are actively looking for leads. That place will be LinkedIn Services, which directly integrates with your LinkedIn profile.

LinkedIn Services' Fee structure

LinkedIn used to charge a monthly fee for their ProFinder service, which was discontinued in Q4, 2021. This new format, called LinkedIn Services, allows you to create a service profile page entirely free.

Ensuring Ongoing Success In Getting Coaching Leads

You will still need to stay involved as leads won't convert themselves to clients. Here are a few things that coaches have shared that gave them great results:

First, sign up to get alerts (via email or the provider's app) so you don't miss a lead request!

Be quick to respond to leads. Statistics show that responses within the first 3 hours of a request are more likely to convert to a client.

Keep your profile updated – schedule time in your calendar for a quarterly check. Make sure you include a professional photo or use your logo. Tailor your profile to address your ideal target audience. You can refer to our guide on identifying your niche in 6 simple steps (including a free worksheet) if you haven't done so already.

Add images and videos that showcase your services and allow your profile visitors to "get to know you" a little. If they like what they see there, they are more likely to request a discovery call with you.

Consider developing a few standard responses that answer the most common questions you receive. Save these responses somewhere to copy and paste them for faster responses. Some platforms allow you to save templates. Thumbtack is a good example. You could include a link to a specific landing page, a link to schedule a free consultation, your signature, or share a free lead magnet or other documents.

Finally, invite clients to submit reviews every time you have worked with them for a while and they are happy. Happy customers are more likely to post a review when they are asked at the time of satisfaction. Coaches found that it's often hard to obtain a review if too much time has passed between your coaching engagement and your request for a testimonial.

Your Coaching Business Starter Checklist

You've done the legwork on the basics. You know your market (niche), the audience (tribe, buyer personas) you are catering to, you can articulate the value you bring, and you have found a great name for your business. What's next?

You may need to refine the items above, so we've added them to the checklist. Cross them off once you are confident with the results. Perhaps run a small survey using the free SurveyMonkey service to ask your friends and family to weigh in on your company name and logo.

The listed options below help make your business operational. This includes actions like setting up a payment account for your business to receive payment from your clients via PayPal, Stripe, etc. View this as a summary of actions based on the previous chapters.

BUSINESS SETUP CHECKLIST

ToDo's	Service or App used	Target Date
✔ *Example: Create Buyer Persona Profile*	*Example: Hubspot*	*Example: End of Q1*
○ Evaluate Coaching Certifications/Schools		
○ Sign up for coach training		
○ Define coaching niche		
○ Create my coaching business pitch		
○ Create buyer persona(s)		
○ Create service offering(s)		
○ Research available business name and website domain		
○ Sign up for a coaching directory/marketplace		
○ Create coaching agreement		
○ Create coaching templates and worksheets		
○ Craft a coaching program		
○ Plan coach operations setup (process/workflow)		
○ Find coaching and business software to support my workflows		
○ Create a communication plan		
○ Create a website		
○ Create social profiles		
○ Get a professional business email		
○ Create content for website		

BUSINESS SETUP CHECKLIST

ToDo's ... continued	Service or App used	Target Date
○ Share business launch with network		
○ Start implementing communication plan		
○ Get business insurance		
○ Obtain coaching certification		
○		
○		
○		
○		
○		
○		
○		
○		
○		
○		
○		
○		
○		
○		
○		
○		

QUESTIONS? JOIN THE COACHING BUSINESS CLINIC!

As a new frontrunner in mentoring coaches, the Coachilly is an online magazine that was established to help you start, establish, and grow a successful coaching business. If you found this guide helpful, subscribe to Coachilly's updates. You'll receive regular advice that is easy to incorporate in day-to-day business, such as the latest updates in coaching tech, industry trends, and regulatory changes.

Don't be shy to ask for help. We have a Business Clinic (closed/private group that is *not* using public social media) and get help for specific challenges you are facing. Don't be shy or feel embarrassed to share your challenges. We talk about lead generation for coaches, client management solutions, business automation, scaling your coaching business, how to create coaching programs, how to create newsletters, how to write emails clients will open (!), and so much more.

The coaches who join these Business Clinics all face similar challenges as you as they build their businesses – we're all learning and growing. The Business Clinic is not a webinar or self-serve training. It's hands-on interaction between you, your peers, and the expert hosts leading it. You bring your challenge, and we'll work through it right then and there, together.

So, don't be shy. Come, ask a question, or share something you've learned. There is no judgment, no grading, and no losing in this private group. Get fired up and enjoy working with committed entrepreneur coaches like you so you can keep going when the going gets hard – and it will get hard at times.

It's essential to keep at it. Refine, practice, and don't give up!

Appendix: Links in this Book

(Organized by Chapter)

1 - What is Professional Coaching?

- IBIS World – Coaching Industry Report: https://www.ibisworld.com/industry-statistics/market-size/business-coaching-united-states/
- Entrepreneur.com Article: "How Entrepreneurs Can Join Europe's Booming Coaching Industry" - https://www.entrepreneur.com/article/348857
- Blog.Marketresearch.com Article: "U.S. Personal Coaching Industry Tops $1 Billion, and Growing" - https://blog.marketresearch.com/us-personal-coaching-industry-tops-1-billion-and-growing
- ICF – International Coach Federation: https://coachingfederation.org
- HCI – Human Capital Institute: https://www.hci.org/about-hci
- 2015 HCI/ICF study, "Building a Coaching Culture for Increased Employee Engagement" - https://www.hci.org/research/building-coaching-culture-increased-employee-engagement
- Clear Coaching Limited 2007 Survey (PDF download): https://www.hci.org/research/building-coaching-culture-increased-employee-engagement
- Article "U.S. Personal Coaching Industry Tops $1 Billion, and Growing" https://blog.marketresearch.com/us-personal-coaching-industry-tops-1-billion-and-growing
- Popular conferencing and training platform providers:
  - Zoom: http://zoom.com/
  - UberConference: http://uberconference.com/
  - Microsoft Teams: https://www.microsoft.com/en-us/microsoft-365/microsoft-teams/group-chat-software
  - FreshLearn: https://coachilly.com/go/freshlearn
  - Teachable: https://teachable.com/
  - Thinkific: http://thinkific.com/
  - Udemy: http://udemy.com/
- Coachilly Article: "The Increased Popularity of Coaching in the Workplace" - https://medium.com/coachilly/coaching-popularity-e55e1534978f
- Tracy Sinclair Article, "The growth and impact of the coaching industry" - https://www.openaccessgovernment.org/the-growth-and-impact-of-the-coaching-industry/88852/
- Hubspot Buyer Persona Profile Development Tool (free): develop a buyer persona profile

- Noomii Coaching Directory: https://www.noomii.com/
- LifeCoachHub: https://coachilly.com/go/lifecoachhub
- Haystack Digital Business Card App: https://thehaystackapp.com/
- Coaching Competencies: https://coachfederation.org/core-competencies
- ROI study on executive coaching: https://gvasuccess.com/articles/ExetutiveBriefing.pdf
- Harvard Business Review comparing three stock portfolios of companies investing in employee development: https://hbr.org/2004/03/hows-your-return-on-people
- International Journal of Evidence Based Coaching and Mentoring: https://radar.brookes.ac.uk/radar/file/2d76c41c-6628-4eed-8a8a-4d0a5c4f5540/1/special11-paper-05.pdf
- Video: Why Bill Gates and Eric Schmitt recommend coaching: https://youtu.be/XLF90uwlI1k
- Book: Trillion Dollar Coach by Eric Schmitt: https://amzn.to/3UbpD0q
- Tim Ferris' interview of Eric Schmitt: https://tim.blog/2019/04/11/the-tim-ferriss-show-transcripts-eric-schmidt-367/
- Coaching Marketplaces: https://coachilly.com/5-places-where-coaches-get-coaching-leads/

ONLINE MEETING AND COLLABORATION PLATFORMS

- Zoom: http://zoom.com/
- UberConference: http://uberconference.com/
- Microsoft Teams: https://www.microsoft.com/en-us/microsoft-365/microsoft-teams/group-chat-software
- Fresh LMS: https://appsumo.8odi.net/ZddbAX
- Teachable: https://appsumo.8odi.net/qav2O
- Thinkific: http://thinkific.com/
- Udemy: http://udemy.com

- Fiverr gig platform: https://coachilly.com/go/fiverr
- Thumbtack: https://coachilly.com/go/thumbtack
- LifeCoachHub: https://coachilly.com/go/lifecoachhub
- Book by Michael E. Gerber, "The E-Myth Revisited:" https://amzn.to/3buZBBu
- Maslow's Hierarchy of Needs: https://www.simplypsychology.org/maslow.html#:~:text=Maslow's%20hierarchy%20of%20needs%20is,hierarchical%20levels%20within%20a%20pyramid.&text=From%20the%20bottom%20of%20the,esteem%2C%20and%20self%2Dactualization.
- Hertzberg's Two-Factor Theory: https://managementstudyguide.com/herzbergs-theory-motivation.htm
- McClelland's Theory of Needs: https://www.mindtools.com/pages/article/human-motivation-theory.htm#:~:text=McClelland's%20Human%20Motivation%20Theory%20states,solve%20problems%20and%20achieve%20goals.
- Vroom's Theory of Expectancy: https://www.sciencedirect.com/topics/social-sciences/expectancy-theory
- McGregor's Theory X and Theory Y: https://www.mindtools.com/pages/article/newLDR_74.htm
- Mark McGuinness in the article: "Key Coaching Skills" - https://www.wishfulthinking.co.uk/2007/06/19/key-coaching-skills/
- Humans Can Make 10,000 Facial Expressions: https://www.discovermagazine.com/mind/the-physiology-of-facial-expressions
- Neuroscience proving that "telling" or teaching doesn't create change in humans: "A Brain Based Approach to Coaching" by Rock Schwartz (PDF download) - https://researchportal.coachfederation.org/Document/Pdf/2886.pdf
- Article, "Salary Range for Professional Job Coaches" - https://work.chron.com/salary-range-professional-job-coaches-3274.html
- September 17, 2020 news release from the U.S. Bureau of Labor Statistics: https://www.bls.gov/news.release/archives/ecec_09172020.htm
- Article, "How Coaches Get Clients" - http://coachilly.com/hot/ten-simple-ways-coaches-get-customers/
- Contract Template Samples: https://www.template.net/business/contracts/basic-contract-template/
- Free, Downloadable CoachAccountable Coaching Templates: https://www.coachaccountable.com/installPackage/YyQYqoIgsnX21pdfRmWxCPBX8TIiU4.

- CoachAccountable Platform Referral: https://coachilly.com/go/coachaccountable
- Article by Umesh Venkatesh on coaching industry statistics: https://www.linkedin.com/pulse/coaching-industry-statistics-umesh-venkatesh/

3 - Business Resources for Coaches

Industry Associations:

- International Coaching Federation (ICF): https://coachingfederation.org
- The International Authority for Professional Coaching and Mentoring (IAPC&M): https://coach-accreditation.services
- The Worldwide Association of Business Coaches (WABC): https://wabccoaches.com/
- Christian Coaching Network (CCN): https://christiancoaches.com/about-ccni/
- The Association for Professional Executive Coaching and Supervision (APECS): https://www.apecs.org/

Coaching Education:

- Institute for Life Coach Training: http://www.lifecoachtraining.com/
- International Association of Professionals (IAP) Career College: https://www.iapcollege.com/program/career-coach-master-professional-certification-course-online/
- Institute for Professional Excellence in Coaches (IPEC): https://www.ipeccoaching.com/
- Institute of Executive Coaching: https://www.iecl.com/coach-education-2023
- CoachU: https://www.coachu.com/home/
- Health Coach Institute: https://www.healthcoachinstitute.com/
- Integrative Wellness Academy: https://iwacoaching.com/
- Professional Christian Coaching Institute (PCCI): https://professionalchristiancoaching.com/
- Radiant Coaches Academy: https://radiantcoachesacademy.com/
- Certified Life Coach Institute: https://www.certifiedlifecoachinstitute.com/
- International Coaching Federation (ICF): https://coachingfederation.org
- The best certification program for Career Coaches: https://coachestoolbox.coachilly.com/career-coaching-business-in-a-box/

Income Expectations for Coaches:

- Salary range: https://work.chron.com/salary-range-professional-job-coaches-3274.html
- Bureau of Labor Statistics: https://www.bls.gov/news.release/archives/ecec_09172020.htm
- How Coaches Get Clients: http://coachilly.com/hot/ten-simple-ways-coaches-get-customers/

INCOME EXPECTATIONS FOR COACHES:

- Core Competencies of Coaches:
  https://coachingfederation.org/app/uploads/2017/12/ICF_Competencies_Level_Table_wNote.pdf

- Neuroscience proof of coaching effectiveness:
  https://researchportal.coachfederation.org/Document/Pdf/2886.pdf

SOFTWARE FOR COACHES:

- Payments:
  - Square: https://coachilly.com/go/squareup
  - Stripe: http://stripe.com/
- Scheduling:
  - Calendly: http://calendly.com/
  - Book Like A Boss: https://coachilly.com/go/boss
  - HubSpot: https://coachilly.com/go/hubspotmeetings
  - TidyCal: https://coachilly.com/go/tidycal
  - Trafft: https://coachilly.com/go/trafft
- Contact Management:
  - Hubspot CRM: https://coachilly.com/go/hubspotcrm
- Newsletter:
  - Sendfox: https://coachilly.com/go/sendfox
  - Constant Contact: https://coachilly.com/go/constantcontact
- Accounting:
  - Quickbooks: https://coachilly.com/go/quickbooks
  - Freshbooks: https://coachilly.com/go/freshbooks
  - Google Sheets: https://www.google.com/sheets/about/
- Marketing:
  - Missinglettr: https://coachilly.com/go/missinglettr
  - Canva: https://coachilly.com/go/canva
  - Carrd: https://carrd.co/
- Automation:
  - Zapier: http://zapier.com/
- Legal / Business Registration:
  - NorthWest Registered Agent: https://coachilly.com/go/northwest
- Conferencing:
  - Zoom: http://zoom.com/
  - UberConference: http://uberconference.com/

- Coaching Software:
  - Article: "Your Ultimate Guide To Buying Great Coaching Software" – https://coachilly.com/2022-coaching-software-comparison/
  - Side-by-side coaching software comparison table: https://docs.google.com/spreadsheets/d/e/2PACX-1vRQbsby5g9z4VBEASsAnWntb8Q3LbudcBL7uHXoEEeXSrHG5xxnCzClSvwrR_NtN-DeTbYhcnQp2tGa/pubhtml?gid=761784146&single=true
  - CoachAccountable: https://coachilly.com/go/coachaccountable
  - Quenza: https://quenza.com
    - Quenza Live Demo: https://youtu.be/6nMrhQP0Agk
    - Quenza detailed review: https://coachilly.com/how-to/quenza-coaching-software-review/
  - Delenta: https://coachilly.com/go/delenta
  - Coaching Loft: https://bit.ly/2IAFJBp
  - Paperbell: https://coachilly.com/go/paperbell
  - SimplyCoach: https://simply.coach
    - SimplyCoach Live Demo: https://youtu.be/EGvJ2_EC_M8?t=76
    - SimplyCoach detailed review: https://coachilly.com/how-to/simply-coach-coaching-software-review/
  - LifeCoachHub: https://coachilly.com/go/lifecoachhub
  - CoachesConsole: http://coachesconsole.com/
  - Coaching.com: https://coachilly.com/coaching-com-review/
  - MyCoachPortal: https://mycoachsolutions.com/my-coach-portal/
  - Coaching Lobby: https://www.coachinglobby.com/
  - Life Coach Office: https://lifecoachoffice.com/
  - Coach Simple: https://www.coachsimple.net/

- Career Coaching Starter Template Pack:
  https://www.coachaccountable.com/installPackage/jDIQeTrJynNWOcKEEH9l2ll
  jJOpcu3

- Wellness Coaching Starter Template Pack:
  https://www.coachaccountable.com/installPackage/0x6Wrq8VOxRx43RZjcHiz
  MakYFmrIo

- Life Coaching Starter Template Pack:
  https://www.coachaccountable.com/installPackage/hn8OrEA9jaCL5njw5ff0Qzr
  isFtz7j

- Finance Coaching Starter Template Pack:
  https://www.coachaccountable.com/installPackage/fgPSTaQ8QnIkrhrOopuFUL
  XwU17cck

- ADHD Coaching Starter Template Pack:
  https://www.coachaccountable.com/installPackage/MTYKxWHxvGnp1sNn484
  6VHcgHXWBBq

- Relationship Coaching Starter Template Pack:
  https://www.coachaccountable.com/installPackage/rDsFRgJNMl6cj6G8s050DG
  cvHKZ0F0

- Coaching Agreement Templates:
  https://www.coachaccountable.com/installPackage/rVbluYGdVIOJ1cP3tauwzm
  P9zV5Uos

4 - Establishing Your Coaching Brand

- Looka (create a logo): https://coachilly.com/go/looka
- The 2021 social media demographics guide: https://khoros.com/resources/social-media-demographics-guide
- Hire a writer: https://coachilly.com/go/fiverr
- Author bio example: https://blog.reedsy.com/author-bio/
- Get a pitch written for your video: https://www.fiverr.com/corinnasdesk
- BigVu (teleprompter): https://coachilly.com/go/bigvu
- Canva (design tool): https://coachilly.com/go/canva
- InVideo (video creation): https://coachilly.com/go/invideo
- Sendfox (create email lists and send newsletters): https://coachilly.com/go/sendfox
- Sproutsocial guide: https://sproutsocial.com/insights/new-social-media-demographics/#instagram-demographics
- 10 free SEO online courses: https://www.reliablesoft.net/free-seo-courses/
- Thumbtack leads: https://coachilly.com/go/thumbtack
- Coaching niche identification: https://coachilly.com/define-coaching-niche/
- Buyer persona tool: https://hubspot.sjv.io/buyer-persona
- Answer The Public: https://answerthepublic.com/
- Book Like A Boss: https://coachilly.com/go/boss
- TidyCal: https://coachilly.com/go/tidycal
- BigVU: https://coachilly.com/go/bigvu
- Canva: https://coachilly.com/go/canva
- Invideo: https://coachilly.com/go/invideo
- Sendfox: https://coachilly.com/go/sendfox
- Find your ideal target client: https://www.hubspot.com/make-my-persona

5 - Finding and Coaching Clients

- Printable, editable worksheets: Coachilly.com/coaching-startup-worksheets — you need to enter the password "start" to access the site
- Business Clinic: https://coachestoolbox.coachilly.com/
- Diapers.com story on Wikipedia: https://en.wikipedia.org/wiki/Diapers.com
- HubSpot's Buyer Persona Creation tool: https://www.hubspot.com/make-my-persona?utm_source=mktg-resources
- Lifecoach.io: https://lifecoach.io
- Thumbtack: https://coachilly.com/go/thumbtack
- Namelix: https://namelix.com/
- NameCheap: https://coachilly.com/go/namecheap
- Godaddy: https://godaddy.com
- NorthWest Registered Agent: https://coachilly.com/go/northwest

- Surveymonkey: https://surveymonkey.com
- Google Forms: https://www.google.com/forms/about/
- Nolo state-by-state business license requirements: https://www.nolo.com/legal-encyclopedia/small-business-license-requirements-a-50-state-guide
- Sole Proprietorship information on Nolo: https://www.nolo.com/legal-encyclopedia/sole-proprietor
- LLC business formation by state on Nolo: https://www.nolo.com/legal-encyclopedia/llc-corporations-partnerships
- C-Corporation information on Nolo: https://www.nolo.com/legal-encyclopedia/corporation
- S-Corporation information on Nolo: https://www.nolo.com/legal-encyclopedia/s-corporations
- S-Corporation Definition on Taxfoundation.org: https://taxfoundation.org/tax-basics/s-corporations/
- C-Corporation Definition on Taxfoundation.org: https://taxfoundation.org/tax-basics/c-corporation-c-corp/
- Pass-through taxation explained on Taxfoundation.org: https://taxfoundation.org/pass-through-businesses/
- Airtable: https://airtable.com/invite/r/En12np3N
- Quickbooks: https://coachilly.com/go/quickbooks
- Subscribe to the Coachilly newsletter: https://sendfox.com/coachilly
- CoSchedule: https://coachilly.com/go/coschedule
- Missinglettr: https://coachilly.com/go/missinglettr
- Publr: https://coachilly.com/go/publr
- Canva: https://coachilly.com/go/canva
- Free Hubspot communication's plan: https://hubspot.sjv.io/CommsPlan
- Noomii Coaching Directory: https://www.noomii.com/
- LifeCoachHub: https://coachilly.com/go/lifecoachhub
- Thumbtack: https://coachilly.com/go/thumbtack
- Coaching.Com: https://www.coaching.com/
- Review of Coaching.com: https://coachilly.com/coaching-com-review/
- LinkedIn Services: https://www.linkedin.com/help/linkedin/answer/130044

Questions? Let's Hear from You!

- Subscribe to Coachilly's updates: https://sendfox.com/coachilly
- Coaching Business Clinic: https://coachestoolbox.coachilly.com

Made in the USA
Middletown, DE
24 April 2024

53444093R00091